ARABIC LITE

ARABIC LITERATURE

An Introduction

SECOND (REVISED) EDITION

BY

H. A. R. GIBB

OXFORD UNIVERSITY PRESS

LONDON OXFORD NEW YORK

Oxford University Press

OXFORD LONDON NEW YORK
GLASGOW TORONTO MELBOURNE WELLINGTON
CAPE TOWN IBADAN NAIROBI DAR ES SALAAM LUSAKA ADDIS ABABA
DELHI BOMBAY CALCUTTA MADRAS KARACHI LAHORE DACCA
KUALA LUMPUR SINGAPORE HONG KONG TOKYO

ISBN 0 19 881332 5

First edition 1926
Second edition 1963

First issued as an Oxford University Press paperback 1974

Printed in Great Britain
at the University Press, Oxford
by Vivian Ridler
Printer to the University

PREFACE TO THE SECOND EDITION

THE first edition of this book was issued in the *World's Manuals* series in 1926. In the intervening thirty-five years not only have some of the writer's views changed under the impact of fuller knowledge and changing angles of approach, but a vastly increased body of Arabic texts has been discovered, described, or published. Even by doubling the length of this new edition it would still be impossible to compass more than a fraction of the output of original works of Arabic writers in poetry and prose. How small a fraction may be judged by comparison with the three supplemental volumes of Carl Brockelmann's bio-bibliographical catalogue (*Geschichte der arabischen Litteratur*), which contain over 2,500 closely packed pages. This, then, remains a selection, and adheres to the aims of the original edition, to indicate the scope of Arabic literature in its entirety and to present in somewhat fuller detail its more purely literary branches. The appendix of translations may, it is hoped, compensate in part for the necessarily brief fragments included in the text, and still more so if it should encourage some readers to discover for themselves some of the pleasures and the wisdom concealed in this half-forgotten segment of the heritage of mankind.

H. A. R. G.

1962

PREFACE TO THE FIRST EDITION

THAT outside the Koran and the *Arabian Nights* there exists an Arabic literature at all is comparatively little known. It has been the aim of this book both to indicate the scope of that literature in its entirety, and to discuss in greater detail its more purely literary branches. So vast a field, with the whole of which few can claim an intimate acquaintance, could only be covered at the cost of some dogmatism and generalization, even in cases where critical opinion is divided. Arabists will at once detect where the work of the eminent Oriental scholars of the last half-century has been laid under contribution; this debt, too large to be indicated throughout the text, is fully acknowledged here. The method of treatment was suggested in the first place by Mr. John de M. Johnson, and the text itself owes much to the kindly criticisms passed on the original draft by Professor Sir Thomas Arnold, on whom, however, no responsibility rests for any heresies that may be found in its pages.

H. A. R. G.

May 1926

CONTENTS

NOTE ON PRONUNCIATION

SINCE this introduction is intended not only for readers with a general interest in literature, but also to meet the needs of students who are beginning the study of Arabic language and culture, it has been necessary to adopt a system of strict transliteration. The Arabic alphabet includes a double series of sibilants and dentals, one series articulated in the front part of the mouth much as in English, the other series 'palatalized', i.e. somewhat in the manner of the second *l* in 'little'. The latter are distinguished by subscript dots (*ḍ*, *ṣ*, *ṭ*, *ẓ*), as well as the 'whispered' *ḥ* in contrast to the *h* in our own usage. For practical purposes these distinctions and their corresponding dots may be disregarded by the general reader. Arabic *q* is a *k* articulated at the back of the mouth, with a hollow sound; it should not be pronounced like our *qu* but rather as in French *cinq*. So also Arabic *gh* resembles a more throaty French *r grasséyé*. Of the two remaining unfamiliar symbols, the glottal stop (') is an interruption of the breath stream giving force to an otherwise initial vowel (as in 'an *ice* house, not a nice house'); the *'ain* sound (') is peculiar to Arabic, and made by vibrating the vocal cords in the throat.

1

INTRODUCTION

CLASSICAL Arabic literature is the enduring monument of a civilization, not of a people. Its contributors were men of the most varied ethnic origins who, nevertheless, under the influence of their Arab conquerors, lost their national languages, traditions, and customs and were moulded into a unity of thought and belief, absorbed into a new and wider Arab nation. The Persians alone, though only after assimilating many of the characteristics and tendencies of the Arabs, succeeded at length in restoring their intellectual and racial independence. Yet even when Arabic was in the eastern provinces displaced from its supremacy by the rise of a Persian literature, it maintained, and has even yet not entirely lost, its position as the universal language of Islamic theology, philosophy, and science. To a greater extent perhaps than the other classical literatures, its flowering was conditional not only upon the existence of a cultured society but also on the liberality and patronage of those in high position. Sharing the historical vicissitudes of the Islamic civilization, it faithfully reflects local political and cultural conditions. Where Muslim society was in decay, literature lost vitality and force, but so long as in one capital or another princes and ministers found pleasure, profit, or reputation in patronizing the arts, the torch was kept burning. So we find that now one land and now another becomes a leading centre of literary culture, until at a period roughly coinciding with the Ottoman conquests in Asia and Africa, and the Renaissance in Europe, the flame, although never extinguished, sinks to a dull glow. The writers of the following centuries, with few exceptions, live on the proceeds of their intellectual patrimony, adding little or nothing to it, while the modern revival of Arabic literature initiated in Syria and Egypt is inspired by another spirit than that of the old classical civilization.

Arabic literature has also shared the fate of the classical literatures in that many valuable works are, it is to be feared, irretrievably lost. As they were dependent for their preservation on a society indifferent, when not actually hostile, to anything outside the narrow range of Islamic theology and its satellite disciplines, it is probable that among the lost works are many which in our eyes would do most honour to the Muslim civilization. There still remains, however, an enormous mass of materials, only partially examined, in scattered manuscripts, out of which the patient labours of European scholars in the nineteenth century, zealously carried on by Arab, Persian, and Indian scholars as well in the present century, have reaped a surprising harvest of long-neglected works of literary or cultural significance. But while practically all extant works of importance are being rapidly made accessible to Arabists, comparatively few of them are at the service of western scholarship in reliable translations, although the number is increasing every year.[1]

As those who could boast pure Arab descent formed but a small minority of those who shared the Islamic

[1] A list of the chief translations into western languages will be found in the bibliography, and the name of every author and book appearing on this list is marked with an asterisk.

civilization, so the Arab himself contributed the smaller proportion of its literature. Nevertheless, it was permeated by modes of thought and expression derived from the country and impressed upon it by the people from which and through whom it issued as a conquering force in the seventh century of our era. Before we can proceed to our main subject, therefore, we must, in this chapter and that which follows, outline the physical and linguistic environment by which Arabic literature was moulded from the outset.

Its birthplace was the sandy plain, partly steppeland, partly desert, of central and north-eastern Arabia. Except in the rare oases the land, bare, monotonous, subject to violent alternations of heat and cold, drought and flood, was, and is, unable to support settled communities. Its inhabitants are of necessity nomadic, subsisting chiefly on the produce of their camels and sheep, and compelled to move unendingly from place to place in search of fresh pasturage. The monotony of their life is broken only by the fierce pleasures of years of plenty and the biting misery of years of famine, and by success or failure in their raids on one another or on the settled communities on their fringes. Their secular physical environment has moulded their habits, thought, and speech, impressing on them those repetitions and abrupt transitions which are reproduced in nearly all aspects of Arab life and literature. The circle of ideas bounding the horizon of such nomads is necessarily narrow; the struggle for existence is too severe to allow of attention to anything beyond the practical and material needs of the day, still less of interest in abstract concepts and religious speculation. Their philosophy is summed up in a number of pithy sayings, their religion is a vague superstition. Their thought is expressed in terms of the concrete, and their language will contain few abstractions beyond those relating to simple activities and physical qualities.

As if to counterbalance this poverty of ideas, the uniformity of life and environment conduces to an exceedingly rich development of language in the realm of material life. Not only do synonyms abound, but every variety of natural phenomenon, however minute, and every separate activity, however complex, is expressed by a term proper to itself. This feature of language may be observed also to a greater or less extent in the speech of other peoples whose nomadic way of life and degree of civilization resembles those of the bedouin of Arabia; but Arabic is unique in having carried over its superluxuriant vocabulary to play an important part in the literature of a highly developed civilization.

The Arabic tongue, however, was not the peculiar possession of the nomads of central and northern Arabia. There existed also settled communities of North Arabs who had come into closer contact with peoples of old-established culture. Between the ancient civilization of the Yemen, in the south-west corner of Arabia, and the frontier districts of Syria and Iraq there were constant commercial relations, which opened a way for cultural influences to penetrate into central Arabia. Along the trade routes substantial communities grew up, as at Mecca, akin in blood and language to the nomads and apparently but little distinguished from them in manners and outlook. At Ḥīra on the Euphrates, where an Arab dynasty reigned under Persian protection, and among the Ghassānid and other tribesmen on the marches of Syria, the Arabs were naturally brought into closer touch with the Christian Aramaic culture. From these sources a thin stream of Aramaic cultural terms found their way into Arabic, but made as little impression on the form and content of the language as the Aramaic culture made on the nomads themselves, condemned by nature to live in primitive simplicity or perish in the struggle for existence.

2

THE ARABIC LANGUAGE

THE ancient languages of south-western Asia, of which Arabic is the youngest and, except for some small remnants and the modern revival of Hebrew, the only living representative, form a well-defined and independent family, known as the Semitic language-group. They are all closely interrelated and present such remarkable affinities in vocabulary and structure that they evidently possess a common origin. Within the family itself, however, there are several groups of dialects marked off by distinctive features, the accepted distribution (omitting minor dialects) being as follows:

A. The language of the Babylonian and Assyrian cuneiform inscriptions, generally known as Accadian, or East Semitic.

B. The ancient languages of Syria and Mesopotamia, collectively termed North or North-western Semitic. These fall into two groups, an earlier and a later:

(*a*) the Canaanite dialects of which Phoenician and Hebrew are the most important;

(*b*) Aramaic, the *lingua franca* of western Asia for many centuries before and after the Christian era, together with Syriac, a Christian literary dialect of north-western Mesopotamia.

C. The languages of Arabia (South or South-western Semitic):

(*a*) Northern Arabic, the literary Arabic of our study;
(*b*) The ancient inscriptional dialects of south Arabia (Sabaean, Minaean, &c.) with their offshoot, Geʿez or Ethiopic, the medieval literary language of Abyssinia.

Many of these languages are little more than different literary dialects, the peculiarities of North Arabic being due, as might be expected, to the uniformity of desert life which, while on the one hand favouring the survival of many of the most primitive elements of the Semitic speech, tended also, as we have seen, towards an excessive elaboration in other respects. The majority of the dialects contain more or less alien elements, but in every case these have been subordinated to the distinctive features which mark off the Semitic languages. Some of these peculiarities, such as their complicated phonetic system and the almost complete absence of compound words, do not concern us here. The outstanding characteristic of the Semitic languages, however, is the root-system, and this we must examine in some detail, as without it several of the special features of Arabic literature would be unintelligible. For in Arabic, as in all other literatures, the canons of wit, elegance, and artistry in writing were dictated by the genius of the language.

Every primary conception in the Semitic languages is expressed by means of consonants only, and the vast majority by three consonants. These three consonants form the root. Primary modifications of the meaning are expressed by internal vowel variations, secondary modifications partly by the same method and partly by affixes and inserted consonants. Thus from the root *QTL*, which conveys the idea of 'Killing', are formed the verb *qatala* (he killed) and the noun *qatl* (killing), the adjectival nouns *qātil* (a killer, with *quttāl* as its plural) and *qatīl* (one killed, pl. *qatlā*), and a number of other derivatives. Conversely every word whose root letters are *QTL* will be connected in some way with the idea of killing. (This is not a universal rule, however; there are many instances in Arabic of two or more concepts sharing a common root; thus *KTB* is connected with both 'writing' and 'assembling'.) This method of narrowing down the signification by intensive construction applies both to nouns and verbs, but whereas in the noun there is an exceedingly wide variety of patterns, the verb has attained to a perfectly rigid system of formal development. From the simple verb (he killed) are formed an intensive (he slaughtered), a causative (he caused to kill or to be killed), and—in South Semitic only—a conative (he tried to kill, he fought with). In the fully developed Arabic scheme each of these again may form a reflexive or middle, and there is in addition a quasi-passive of the simple form besides proper passives for each form. Few verbs possess the entire scheme, but nearly all roots receive some or other of these modifications, often with considerable semantic shifts.

It will be clear that, since the verbal scheme is invariable and admits of no exceptions, and since roots are all of three consonants, there exists in Arabic an enormous number of words whose vowel-schemes are exactly alike. Every noun of agent from the simple verb, for example, is formed exactly like *qātil*: *rākib* (a rider), *kātib* (a writer), *ḥāmil* (a carrier), &c. Inevitably, therefore, rhyme and assonance play a very large part in Arabic literary style from the first, not only in poetry but in prose as well, and alliteration and *jeux de mots*, so far from being avoided, are regarded as special ornaments in belles-lettres.

The intensive modification of the root lends itself peculiarly to economy of words, and the most admired form of expression is the concise and pregnant sentence. Arabic proverbs rarely exceed three or four words, and poets were judged by their ability to pack a complete picture into a single line. That 'Oriental floweriness', which has become a byword, is foreign to natural Arabic expression and crept into later Arabic literature from external sources. Yet Arabic took to it kindly, and the rank luxuriance of its later phases was due to the unequalled opportunities for literary artifice which Arabic provided by its wealth of synonyms and the delicate distinctions in meaning offered by its variety of derivations. The older and more natural laconic turn of phrase, however, persisted and still persists in the spoken language and some departments of literature.

Yet, given all these natural foundations, there remains something strange and even inexplicable in the artistic literary structure of Arabic. Everything indicates that there was a wide variety of tribal dialects in Arabia, which in their spoken forms preserved the looseness of traditional Semitic syntax. While the Indo-European languages developed an elaborate scheme of tenses, the Semitic verb had retained the more primitive organization into two 'aspects', which primarily carry no connotation of time but denote simply that the action is completed or incomplete. The modal system of the Indo-European languages also is largely absent from the Semitic languages in general. Thus the word *yaqtulu* expresses not only 'he kills', 'he will kill', and (in composition) 'he was killing', but also 'he may, might, would, or could kill', the exact force of the word being determined by the context. Furthermore, the presentation of the sentence is jerky or 'lyrical'; the component parts are originally autonomous, and seldom explicitly subordinated as in the ordered hierarchy of European syntax.

In striking contrast to all this, the language of the early poets is, with a few minor exceptions, largely uniform in vocabulary, and absolutely so in morphology and syntactical refinement. There is a precise tense structure for principal clauses, and a delicate modal system operated by case-endings. Superimposed on the original autonomy of the component clauses is a scheme of logical subordination, perfectly uniform in its application and capable of expressing every relationship between the clauses. How this linguistic instrument, rich and flexible beyond anything known in other Semitic languages, was evolved, and how it was related to the spoken dialects of the tribes, remains an unsolved problem. Centuries later it became a dogma that the poets had adopted the dialect of the tribe to which Muḥammad belonged, the Quraish of Mecca, as the purest and most evolved of the peninsular dialects; but this theory, patently the offspring of religious piety, cannot be upheld. The conclusion that emerges from discussion hitherto is that the poets used a standardized poetic idiom based on the spoken dialects but distinguished from them by refinements of vocabulary, inflection, and syntactical articulation. The theory of an *artificial* poetic dialect is untenable for many reasons. It is probable, however, that the poets greatly enriched the language by absorption of dialect forms, that they helped to fix its usages, and thus created a standard of cultured speech which came to be called *al-ʿarabīya* (literally 'the bedouin idiom'), and which we shall designate as 'High Arabic'. Once established, it remained the medium of all later literary production, although somewhat simplified in vocabulary in what has been called the *koiné* of the 'Golden Age' and the following centuries.

For the western student, learning to read classical Arabic is a considerable adventure. The semantic twists of the already luxuriant Arabic vocabulary, both in its earliest stages and in later times, are bewildering, and the unfamiliar methods of articulating ideas even more so, until he has acquired a thorough grasp of the inner mechanisms that define their relations. He has, moreover, to decipher all this in the Arabic script, a beautiful cursive script capable of a great variety of artistic modellings, but full of traps for the unwary (not to speak of textual errors resulting from the ignorance or carelessness of copyists or printers). Since the consonantal structure of the words and the general syntactical order are regarded as sufficient to determine the sense, it is not considered necessary to insert the vowels in writing. Hence, as it has been put, an Arabic text contains only seventy-five per cent. of the meaning and the remaining twenty-five per cent. has to be supplied by the reader. But with the realization at a very early date by the Arabs themselves that the text of the Koran must be preserved from corruption or misunderstanding, a system of vowel signs was devised, inserted above or below the letters of the consonantal text. By their use the Arabic script can be rendered at will completely phonetic, although in practice only the Koran and quotations from it, and sometimes poetry, are regularly vocalized. In normal prose style the great majority of the difficulties disappear as soon as the reader has learned the conventions that underlie its structure. It is true that in some old classical texts one can identify every word in a sentence and understand its syntactical construction, and yet hesitate between two widely different interpretations.

In addition, the Arabic poet or scholar, an Abū Tammām or an Abu'l-ʿAlā, and even some modern writers, take what seems at times a perverse pleasure in challenging their readers' wit and erudition. Most of the classics of Arabic literature, however, have come down to us with extensive philological commentaries by the medieval scholars. These, with their apparatus of variants, do not, to be sure, eliminate all problems, but they provide a solid basis for scholarly study and literary appreciation.

3

THE HEROIC AGE

(*c.* A.D. 500–622)

THE most striking feature in Arabic literature is its unexpectedness. Over and over again, with scarcely a hint to give warning of what is coming, a new literary art emerges fully-fledged, often with a perfection never equalled by later exponents of the same art. Nowhere is this element of surprise more striking than in the first appearance of Arabic as a vehicle of literature. At one moment Arabia seems, in a literary sense, empty and dumb except for some votive or businesslike inscriptions in a variety of dialects. At the next, companies of poets spring up all over northern Arabia, reciting complex odes, *qaṣīdas*, in which a series of themes are elaborated with unsurpassed vigour, vividness of imagination, and precision of imagery, in an infinitely rich and highly articulated language, showing little or no traces of dialect, and cast into complex and flexible metrical schemes that rhyme throughout the poem.

The Arabic philologists of later times share our feeling of surprise. 'The early Arabs [says Ibn Sallām, one of the earliest and best of Arabic critics] had no poetry other than verses spoken by some person or other on certain occasions. *Qaṣīdas* and long poems were first recited in the time of 'Abd al-Muṭṭalib', that is, in the first half of the sixth century. So far as the themes are concerned, no doubt most of these were already the subjects of those 'verses spoken by some person or other'. Elegies, laments, boasting-poems, satires or cursing-poems, praises of horse or camel, war-poems and the like must have existed long before. Many such short pieces have come down to us from a period contemporary with the early *qaṣīdas*, and justify the assumption that they existed as separate themes of occasional verse. But the problem of the metres is more complex. The old Arabic primitive metre was a loose iambic form called *rajaz*, consisting of short rhyming lines, probably developed (like the *carmen*) out of brief comminatory utterances in rhymed prose (*saj'*) which were thought to possess magical powers—a conception familiar to us from the story of Balaam. But between this loose poetical form, common to all the Semitic literatures, and the ten or twelve metres of sixth-century poetry there is no apparent connexion, and no other Semitic language has anything resembling the latter, except by imitation. The exclusion of *rajaz* from the permissible metres employed in the *qaṣīda* indicates a conscious dissociation of it from the new metres. Many theories have been tentatively suggested for their origin, but while it may be reasonably certain that they did not originate with the *qaṣīda* they probably do not greatly antedate it.

It would seem from all this that the *qaṣīda* represents the culmination of a period of poetical experiment, during which the new metres were discovered and standardized. But it is more than this; it is the expression of a new sense of power in poetical composition, of delight and exultation in the new ranges of aesthetic sensibility that were opened up by this discovery. There is no *rajaz* poem, whether of earlier or later times, that can compare with the sense of uplift that they give. The germ, or the stimulus, may have come from contacts with the cultures of the Fertile Crescent, but there is no evidence as yet to support the suggestion. In any case, the new metres fit the structure of Arabic speech with extraordinary rightness and harmonic adjustment. From this came that astonishing outburst of poetic talent, spreading within a period of a few years or decades among all the tribes of Arabic speech, from Mesopotamia through Najd and the Ḥijāz, and down into the wild ranges of ʿAsīr, and finally into Yemen. It called out powers hitherto latent; for while the uniformity of Arabic morphology and the natural flow of the speech-forms into the new metrical patterns made it easy to compose a few rhyming lines, it took a high poetical talent to expand the poem to sixty or eighty lines and to preserve throughout the same level of artistic and technical accomplishment.

The final object of the *qaṣīda* is self-praise, eulogy of the poet's tribe, satire directed at rival groups or individuals, or panegyric of a patron. But before reaching his climax the poet seeks to build up a favourable climate of emotional reactions among his audience by a series of preliminary themes on various aspects of Arabian life. The strangest of these to us is the conventional opening theme, technically called *nasīb*.

In the opening lines the poet is supposed to be travelling on a camel with one or two companions. The road leads him to the site of a former encampment of his own or a friendly tribe, the remains of which are still visible. He beseeches his companions to halt for a moment, and sorrowfully recalls how, many years ago, he spent here the happiest days of his life with his beloved. Now life with its constant wanderings has separated them, and over the deserted scene roams the wild antelope.[1]

[1] Freely after I. Kratchkowsky, *Vostok*, iv. 101.

Stay! let us weep, while memory tries to trace
The long-lost fair one's sand-girt dwelling-place;
Though the rude winds have swept the sandy plain,
Still some faint traces of that spot remain.
My comrades reined their coursers by my side,
And 'Yield not, yield not to despair' they cried.
(Tears were my sole reply; yet what avail
Tears shed on sands, or sighs upon the gale?)[1]

This theme, which is often called erotic, is in fact something quite different. It is an elegiac reminiscence of love; its essential emotional element is the evocation of parting, and it has little in common with the love-poem or *ghazal*, no example of which is to be found in what has come down to us of pre-Islamic poetry. Passages of erotic description occasionally occur, but they are clearly distinguished from the *nasīb*-theme. The *nasīb* itself has a function only in relation to the *qaṣīda*; as the philologist Ibn Qutaiba tells us, it is introduced only 'to incline the hearts of the poet's hearers towards him and to call out their rapt attention', and should thus have come into existence only with the new organization of the ode. Ibn Sallām, indeed, in his catalogue of reasons for the pre-eminence of Imru' ul-Qais, credits him with the invention of the 'deserted-encampment' theme. Whether justly ascribed to him or not, there can be no doubt that the theme possessed an enduring appeal for the Arab poet and his audience; however stereotyped its formulation in the *nasībs* of later and post-Islamic poets, the repeated allusion to it in a variety of later contexts (for example on p. 111 below) bears evidence to its strong emotional associations.

After depicting the final separation from his beloved as

[1] From a translation of the *Muʿallaqa* of Imru'ul-Qais quoted by Clouston, *Arabian Poetry*, p. 373.

her tribe moves off to seek fresh pastures, the poet pursues his journey and seizes the occasion to describe, sometimes briefly but often with all an expert's enthusiasm, the fine points of his camel or horse. Its swiftness and endurance of fatigue on his long and dangerous journeys leads him to compare it to a wild ass, ostrich, or oryx, but the comparison often seems to become submerged as the theme is developed into a lively picture of animal life or of a hunting scene, which to western taste is often the most attractive section of the poem.

She, the white cow, shone there through the dark night luminous, like a pearl of deep-seas, freed from the string of it,
Thus till morn, till day-dawn folded back night's canopy; then she fled bewildered, sliding the feet of her. . . .
Voices now she hears near, human tones, they startle her, though to her eye naught is: Man! he, the bane of her!
Seeketh a safe issue, the forenoon through listening, now in front, behind now, fearing her enemy.
And they failed, the archers. Loosed they then to deal with her fine-trained hounds, the lop-eared, slender the sides of them.
These outran her lightly. Turned she swift her horns on them, like twin spears of Sámhar, sharp-set the points of them.
Well she knew her danger, knew if her fence failed with them hers must be the red death. Hence her wrath's strategy.
And she slew Kasábi, foremost hound of all of them, stretched the brach in blood there, ay, and Sukhám of them.[1]

Only after this, as a rule, does the poet break into the subject proper of his poem. By the use of carefully

[1] From the *Mu'allaqa* of Labīd, in W. S. Blunt's *Seven Golden Odes*. In this passage both the phrasing and rhythm of the Arabic are closely followed.

selected epithets he unfolds to his audience a series of idealized portraits of tribal life, a scene of revel, or a desert thunderstorm; he extols his own bravery or defiantly proclaims the glorious deeds of his tribe and the disgrace of its rivals or enemies; he sings the praises of his patron and lauds his generosity; in exultant tones he describes a battle or a successful raid; or he sums up the ethics of the desert in a vein of didactic pessimism. Thus the *qaṣīd*-poets incorporated into their art practically the entire repertory of subjects of the older poetry with the single exception of the elegy. This long preserved its own traditional structure, and is remarkable also for several poetesses who excelled in it, the most celebrated being *al-Khansā' of the tribe of Sulaim, in west-central Arabia. Her elegies for her brother Ṣakhr, killed in battle about 615, were famed throughout Arabia, and legend delights to display the poetess intervening in poetic tournaments at 'Ukāẓ in the company of famous poets.

The *qaṣīda*, once established as the acme of poetic genius, became the standard by which the quality of a poet was judged. But now there set in a second process, which is equally characteristic of Arabic literature in its later development. Once a literary form is established, it remains henceforward standardized and almost stereotyped in its main lines. The earliest poems, presumably addressed to the poet's fellow tribesmen, are loose in the choice and order of their themes, and seem to have no function but to express the poet's own personality and reactions to his circumstances. But this very soon changed. One result of the development of the new poetic art was that poetry began to become a profession. At first, something survived of the old conception of the *shu'arā*, 'kenners', as wielders of rhythmic words which exerted magical powers, and there are numerous stories of the inspiration of poets by heavenly beings or demons (*jinn*). The great poets, however, no longer devote themselves to extempore productions on the battlefield or other minor occasions; they reserve their powers for poetic tournaments, at seasons when different tribes come together for fairs or pilgrimages, or for recitation before the kings of Ḥīra and Ghassān or other great chiefs. A profession requires a clientèle, and the clientèle signifies its approval not only by platonic appreciation but by tangible recompense of herds and other possessions.

This had a considerable effect in standardizing the structure of the *qaṣīda*. To gain approval the poet had not only to play up to the tribal sense of pride or to his patron's self-importance; he was obliged even more to keep within the range of themes which his audience understood, trying to touch their feelings and captivate them by an allusive and pictorial evocation of subjects with which they were familiar and on which they were ready to back their judgement. He could not, even had he wished, strike out on fresh paths and introduce a new or wider range of ideas; had he done so, he would have outstripped their comprehension and lost contact with them.

Another result of the development of poetry as a profession contributed also to the stereotyping of the *qaṣīda*. This was the growth of a system of apprenticeship to the new profession. A famous poet had in his train one or more acolytes, *rāwīs*, 'reciters', who learned his productions by heart and transmitted them to others, so that they passed from mouth to mouth over a wider or narrower range of territory. Once a *rāwī* had learned the technical secrets of handling the *qaṣīda*, he might well become a poet on his own account, but with an almost inevitable diminution of spontaneity and substitution of conscious art. One *rāwī*, at least, became a greater poet than his master, namely Zuhair, the *rāwī* of Aws b. Ḥajar. But it is precisely Zuhair and his school whom the Arabic philologists regarded as typical 'slaves of poetry', because of their excessive addiction to technique as against the productions of the 'poets by nature'.

In course of time, however, *rāwīs* themselves became a class of professional reciters with a wide general repertoire, and the survival of the ancient poetry for some two centuries, until its fixation in writing, was due entirely to their transmission of it. Many stories are related of the prodigious memories of certain famous *rāwīs*, one of whom is said to have recited on one occasion 2,900 long poems at a single sitting. Such stories, however, carry their own question-marks with them. Was it really possible, given the utmost good faith of the *rāwīs*, to preserve the authentic original texts over so long a period from errors, revisions, some polishing here or there, or (especially in view of the rather loose articulation of the Arabian ode) from omissions or misplacements? Might not reciters make mistakes over authorship, attributing poems to the wrong poet, or transferring verses with like metre and rhyme from one poem to another? Most of the old Arabian poetry relates to specific tribal events and personages, and is fully intelligible only when these are known; as they passed out of living memory, the poems connected with them would either drop out of currency or be reconnected to some other traditional story-cycle and possibly remodelled to fit it. Most disturbing of all, what guarantee could there be that ambitious and jealous *rāwīs* might not pass off poems of their own composition or of some obscure poet as the productions of some famous poet of the past? The philologists who collected the old poetry in the eighth century were, however, well awake to these questions, perhaps even excessively so, to judge by the accusations of forgery freely bandied about between rival collectors and schools. A few modern critics have gone even further, and on the ground of these mutual accusations or other hypotheses have denied the genuineness of the whole body, or of all but a fraction, of pre-Islamic Arabic poetry. But this is hypercriticism. We shall see later that it would have been impossible for *rāwīs* of the eighth century, if they had nothing behind them but the undoubtedly genuine productions of the seventh, to have imagined the markedly different poetry of the pre-Islamic age, and to have invented all its particular local and personal diversities. While it may very seldom be possible to provide objective evidence for the authenticity of any given poem with complete certitude, nevertheless (and notwithstanding all possible sources of error, verbal modification, or re-arrangement) there can be no doubt that the commonly accepted nucleus of poems ascribed to the poets of the sixth century is a faithful reproduction of their poetic output and technique, and thus substantially authentic. Most, indeed, of what must have been an immense volume of poetry has perished, but what survives includes, at least, all those works which have been most highly esteemed by every generation of native critics.

The general similarity in structure and content of the pre-Islamic odes may give, especially when they are read in translation, an impression of monotony, almost of bareness, mirroring with a certain rude force the uniformity of desert life, its concreteness, realism, absence of shading and of introspection. Where the poet is held almost wholly to specific themes, and his aim is to embellish those themes with all the art at his command, to surpass his predecessors and rivals in beauty, expressiveness, terseness of phrase, in fidelity of description and grasp of reality, then such poetry can never be satisfactorily translated into any other language, just because the thing said varies so little and the whole art lies in the untranslatable manner of saying it.

But it would be utterly wrong to leave the impression that all the poets followed the same mould, or reserved their powers solely for panegyrics. One need not look further than the famous collection called the **Mu'allaqāt*,[1] an anthology of seven 'Golden Odes' made by a *rāwī* of the eighth century, to which three other odes are commonly appended. The ten poems are by as many hands, the masters of pre-Islamic poetry, and each is regarded as its author's masterpiece. No two of them are alike, and only one is an outright panegyric, that of Zuhair, most of whose *dīwān* (i.e. collected poetical works) is devoted to the praises of two chiefs for composing a fratricidal feud, and who, with the wisdom of age, stands out as the mouthpiece of the pessimistic ethics of the desert. The *mu'allaqa* of his fellow tribesman Nābigha is a half-defiant apology mingled with panegyric addressed to the king of the Arab state of Ḥīra on the Euphrates (see p. 4 above), of whom he was almost the court poet—the first example of this practice in Arabic literature.

Two others are addressed to an earlier king of Ḥīra by poets of rival tribal groups. 'Amr ibn Kulthūm, the spokesman of the tribe of Taghlib, who ranged the north-eastern quarter of the Syrian desert, presents any-

[1] The term, which literally means 'suspended', has not yet been satisfactorily explained. A story of later concoction asserts that they were the winning poems at poetic tournaments held at the fair of 'Ukāẓ, transcribed in gold and hung up in the Ka'ba at Mecca.

thing but a panegyric; rather it is one of the most uncompromising expressions of tribal pride and defiance:

With what intent, O ʿAmr son of Hind, do you scorn us,
  And follow the whim of those who embroider against us?
With what intent, O ʿAmr son of Hind, are *we* to be made
  Domestics under the thumb of your little kinglet?
Be sparing in menace, go gently with threats against us—
  When, pray, did *we* come to be your mother's minions?
Our spearshafts, O ʿAmr, are tough, and have foiled the efforts
  Of enemies ere your time to cause them to bend.

and ends with an extravagant climax of boasts:

To us belongs the earth and all who dwell thereon;
  When we despoil, resistless is our swoop. . . .
The mainland grows too narrow for our swelling hosts,
  The sea is ours, we fill it with our ships.

The poem of his opponent, al-Ḥārith ibn Ḥilliza of the tribe of Bakr on the lower Euphrates, is a rather less successful combination of boasting and satire, and patronizingly panegyrical towards King ʿAmr ibn Hind.

The rest are mainly poems of self-praise. First in point of time and also, in the opinion of many critics, in poetic merit is the *muʿallaqa* of Imru 'ul-Qais, the dissolute and exiled son of the ruler of a precarious north-Arabian kingdom, and 'leader of the poets to hell-fire' in the eyes of early Muslim puritanism. His poem is entirely self-centred, and noted for its natural descriptions, including a fine picture of a thunderstorm, as well as for the frankness of his amatory passages. The same self-centredness is found in the poems of ʿAntara, slave-born hero of the tribe of ʿAbs, and the Bakrite Ṭarafa, the former vaunting his prowess in the battlefield, the latter chiefly concerned with the fine points of his she-camel and his prowess in the tavern.

The two latest, Labīd and al-Aʿshā, are professional troubadours, belonging to the last generation of pre-Islamic poets, and seem already to show signs of the growing standardization of technique and themes. The former specializes in scenes of animal life, the latter in reminiscences of love and drinking, leading ultimately in both to boasting of their own exploits and that of their tribes, or to panegyric.

Altogether some hundreds of *qaṣīdas* have come down to us, more or less authenticated. In addition to the *dīwāns* of the ten poets of the *Muʿallaqāt* and of several others, another collection, contemporary with the *Muʿallaqāt* and named after its compiler (the philologist al-Mufaḍḍal) the **Mufaḍḍalīyāt*, contains some 120 odes and fragments, chiefly from lesser pre-Islamic poets, and there are several other collections of less celebrity. But it would be a mistake to confine our attention exclusively to *qaṣīdas*. Although the ode represents the culmination of the poetic art in Arabia, it by no means constituted the greater part of its poetic production. Alongside it there existed a vast output of shorter poems, elegies, impromptus, &c., which, less convention-bound than the *qaṣīda*, must also enter into any reckoning of the measure and quality of the poetic genius of the Arabs. Most of these have come down in anthologies of excerpts and occasional pieces, the most famous being the **Dīwān al-Ḥamāsa* (Poems of Bravery), compiled by Abū Tammām (p. 85), himself a poet of note in the ninth century. The collection, which has been rendered in spirited German verse by Rückert, is divided into ten sections, the first and longest of which has given its name to the work. Another anthology bearing the same title was made by the poet al-Buḥturī (p. 85) some years later. Many excerpts from the ancient poems are contained also in the *Kitāb al-Aghānī* (Book of Songs) of Abu'l-Faraj al-Iṣfahānī (d. 967), a valuable collection in twenty volumes of biographies of poets and musicians, from which most of our knowledge of ancient Arabian society and manners is drawn, and in numerous works of philology and belles-lettres. No one who reads the poems preserved in the *Ḥamāsa* of Abū Tammām (or the pieces translated from it by Sir Charles Lyall) will deny that here is an art, springing out of natural feeling and popular consciousness, and expressing with vigour, with a certain wild beauty, and often with a strangely moving power, the personality of the poets and the conceptions and ideals of their age.

If, however, we ask what it is that gives this poetry its appeal for us, its 'universality', it is not easy to give a clear and definite answer. For its own people in its own time, a modern Arabic critic has said, 'it satisfied its hearers because it expressed their own passions and emotions, and portrayed their lives as individuals and as a society forcefully and truthfully'. But its appeal lies far more in the fact that, in holding the mirror up to life, it presented an image larger than life. The passions and emotions and portrayals were idealized in content and expression—in content because it presented the Arabs to themselves as they would have liked to be, immeasurably bold and gallant and openhanded, and in expression because these ideal images were clothed in rich, sonorous, and evocative language, and given emotional intensity by the beating rhythms and ever-recurring rhyme.

Yet to emphasize exclusively the linguistic artistry of the poet and the realism and naturalism of his subjects, however elevated by imagery and decoration, is to miss one essential element of his craft. All of these subserved his main purpose, so to stimulate the imaginative response of his audience that the poem becomes a dialogue between them, a dialogue in which the audience are alert to grasp the hints and allusions compressed within the compass of his verse and to complete his portrait or thought for themselves. Thus no line of panegyric in pre-Islamic poetry is more celebrated than one of Nābigha in praise of the Ghassānid princes of Transjordan:

No fault in them but that their sword-blades
Are notched from beating on the mailèd squadrons.

Or again when, in a different mode, he praises his patron, the king of Ḥīra:

No, not Euphrates itself with its crests in flood,
  As its foaming breakers cover its banks with spume,
And every clamorous torrent gushes to join it,
  Bearing its wrack of herbage and splintered boughs,
While the frightened sailor clings to his rudder-oar,
  Spent with fatigue yet straining to hold his course,
Can outdo in abundance his unmeasured bounty,
  Nor does his gift today stand in the way of tomorrow.

This is realism with a difference. In that heightening of the reality, that idealizing of the common incidents and aspirations of life, that challenge by image and allusion to the understanding and intelligence of the hearer, lie the elements that transform the poet's words from the stuff of prose to the stuff of poetry, and give them their appeal even to our aesthetic feeling. Only after this do the adornments of language come in to add to their effect. One needs no knowledge of Arabic to appreciate the almost physical excitement created among an audience of parched nomads by the cumulation of similes in such a passage as:

'Twas then her beauties first enslaved my heart—
Those glittering pearls and ruby lips, whose kiss
Was sweeter far than honey to the taste.
As when a merchant opes a precious box
Of perfume, such an odour from her breath
Came toward thee, harbinger of her approach;
Or like an untouched meadow, where the rain
Hath fallen freshly on the fragrant herbs
That carpet all its pure untrodden soil:
A meadow where the frequent rain-drops fall
Like coins of silver in the quiet pools,
And irrigate it with perpetual streams;
A meadow where the sportive insects hum
Like listless topers singing o'er their cups.[1]

To distinguish the personality of the poets calls for an even more complex analysis and intensive study of detail, already difficult for the medieval Arabic critics. In a certain sense all Arabic odes of more than mediocre quality are subjective, but in differing manner and degrees. The productions of those poets whom we have called self-centred are more obviously so, and this self-centredness finds, as might be expected, its most intense expression in the robber or outlaw poets such as, to name only the most famous, *Ta'abbaṭa Sharrā and *ash-Shanfarā. The sharp and staccato *Song of Revenge* of the former is one of the best known and most often translated of Arabic poems.[2] In another piece he portrays in terse and pungent outline his own ideal:[3]

[1] From the *mu'allaqa* of 'Antara, translated by E. H. Palmer in *The Song of the Reed*.

[2] C. J. Lyall, *Translations from Ancient Arabian Poetry*, pp. 48–51.

[3] Translated by W. G. Palgrave, *Essays on Eastern Questions*, p. 312; and cf. Lyall, op. cit., p. 16.

Nor exults he nor complains he; silent bears whate'er befalls him,
Much desiring, much attempting; far the wanderings of his venture.
In one desert noon beholds him; evening finds him in another;
As the wild ass lone he crosses o'er the jagged and headlong ridges.
Swifter than the wind unpausing, onward yet, nor rest nor slackness,
While the howling gusts outspeeded in the distance moan and falter.
Light the slumber on his eyelids, yet too heavy all he deems it;
Ever watchful for the moment when to draw the bitter faulchion,
When to plunge it in the heart-blood of the many-mustered foemen.

Ash-Shanfarā's *Poem rhyming in L* (*Lāmīyat al-ʿArab*) is an even more powerful composition, a unique concentration of exact observations and experiences of desert life, compressed into a language of extreme tautness, and with sombre undertones of bitterness, savage resentment, and covert satire of the smug tribal communities and their pampered poets.

The great majority of *qaṣīd*-poets, however, can express their personalities only in muted form, subordinated as they are not only to the conventions of their craft, but also within these limits held to the expression of the collective thought and feeling rather than their own intuitions. Nevertheless, the poet aims to centre all descriptions and ancillary themes upon his personal vision; he may not transcend the conventions, but in his imaginative handling of his topics, his degree of realism and modes of idealization, he gives them fresh meaning and value in terms of his personal insights.

Imru 'ul-Qais describes the storm, for example; but however naturalistic the detail it is presented in terms of his own observation, and the massing of the effects is as truly his as on a painter's canvas. Yet even this degree of subjectivity is sometimes difficult to find in many *qaṣīdas*, and it is not surprising that the absence of personality may sometimes create a feeling that it is all a mechanical exercise and indeed nothing more than clever literary forgery.

But there is also the other side of the picture to be borne in mind. Such an art-poetry could never have come into existence, nor have developed its technique of imaginative interplay between poet and audience, unless the audiences too were gifted with peculiar aesthetic sensibilities. Even down to the present day, the apt use of words has remained the supreme art of the Arabs, exerting upon them an almost uncontrollable emotive power, and the inexhaustible richness of their language is a source of pride. Among the pre-Islamic Arabs, words in themselves seem to have retained something of their ancient mystical and magical power; the man who, by skilful ordering of vivid imagery in taut, rightly nuanced phrases, could play upon the emotions of his hearers, was not merely lauded as an artist but venerated as the protector and guarantor of the honour of the tribe and a potent weapon against its enemies. Tribal contests were fought out as much, or more, in the taunts of their respective poets as on the field of battle, and so deeply rooted was the custom that even Muḥammad, although in general hostile to the influence of the poets, himself conformed to it in his later years at Madīna.

In view of such a universal veneration of the poetic art, it is not after all surprising that the productions of the great *qaṣīd*-poets were handed down from generation to generation. It was, again, not merely that they set the linguistic and aesthetic standards which were to dominate almost all Arabic poetry (and much of its prose as well) down to the modern age; but they fulfilled also another function, by no means less important. Poetry, said the later philologists, was 'the *dīwān* of the Arabs'; it preserved the collective memory of the past, and so gave an element of continuity and meaning to the otherwise fleeting and insubstantial realities of the present. In the two major themes of eulogy and satire the poets pressed home the moral antitheses and sanctions by which this collective existence was regulated and sustained. With relatively few exceptions, the pre-Islamic poets express, and even prescribe, a high standard of tribal morality, and noticeably avoid any reference to the humbler and ruder features of bedouin life and its environment.

We must not forget, however, that the population of Arabia did not consist exclusively of bedouins. Both the agricultural Judaized tribes in the Ḥijāz and the other settlements and towns also had their poets, and we catch glimpses of a body of religious poetry and of drinking-songs at Ḥīra itself. The latter had some influence on the Arabic poetry of the next century, but in general the poetry of the sedentaries was regarded as inferior, and little of it has survived.

Finally, the most important cultural service which the poets rendered was their creation of a common standard of High Arabic, which as an instrument transcended narrow tribal limits, sharply distinguished Arab from non-Arab or metic, and thus supplied the substrate for a new consciousness of Arab nationhood. Although there is no evidence that the poets themselves consciously propagated it, this new national consciousness needed only a spark to awaken it. Once the spark was supplied by Islam, it was to find expression in the great movement of expansion that broke out with startling suddenness when the cities, with their greater powers of organization, supplied the cohesive force which was so marked a deficiency in the tribal society.

4

THE AGE OF EXPANSION

(A.D. 622–750)

THE influences which were being brought to bear on the nomads through the poets were active also in the towns, but in a different fashion. While the townsmen preserved the primitive clan organization, they had gained a wider outlook through their economic activities, and especially in commercial intercourse with the north and the south. The trading centres of the Ḥijāz and of Najd were the natural foci for the cultural elements that were invading the peninsula. Christian and Jewish propaganda were at work also to strengthen the impressions made upon them by their contacts with the civilized world. The poetry of Umayya ibn Abi'ṣ-Ṣalt of Ṭā'if, the sister-city of Mecca, even if open to question in part, expresses the dissatisfaction felt by thoughtful men with the barren superstitions of their ancestors.

While the settlements of Najd exercised at most only an indirect influence on Arabic literature, at Mecca the reform movement broke through in the teachings of Muḥammad ibn ʿAbdallāh, a member of one of the clans of its mercantile aristocracy, the Quraish. His life has been so overlaid by later traditions that little is known of him prior to the opening of his mission. He had lived as a child among the nomads and as a young man had visited Syria with the trading caravans. In middle life he seems to have given himself up to deep and often solitary meditations over a long period of years. At length he felt called to proclaim to his fellow citizens his profound conviction of the power and majesty of the One God and of the impending judgement when all who had rebelled against His laws should be cast into the fire of Hell. After ten years of continuing struggle he had succeeded in collecting only a small band of followers, when an opportune invitation to compose the feuds that were raging in the town of Yathrib offered a new field of action. In 622, a date that became the era of the new community, already known as Muslims, he with the bulk of the followers made his emigration (*hijra*) to Yathrib, henceforth to be known as Madīnat an-Nabī, the City of the Prophet. For eight years he maintained an armed struggle with Mecca and the bedouin tribes of north-west Arabia, imposing his authority on one after another until at length Mecca itself capitulated in 630. In the two years of life that remained to him his rule was undisputed in western Arabia, and deputations from all parts of the peninsula flocked to Madīna to tender their submission or enlist his aid in the factional conflicts that rent their tribes.

It was not until after his death that his followers finally compiled his discourses, largely from memory, into a single volume, known as the Koran (*al-Qur'ān*, the original meaning of which seems to have been 'the Lectionary'). No serious doubt has ever been cast on the authenticity of the collection, the very haphazardness of the compilation, apart from internal evidence, being a proof of its genuineness. Except for certain broadly coherent sections, little attempt was made to arrange the fragments, either chronologically or in order of content; earlier and later passages, moral discourses, and legal provisions, are placed side by side even in the same chapter (*sūra*). Both Muslim and western scholars have set themselves the task of determining the chronological order of the passages, and it is now possible to re-arrange them with a fair approximation to certainty.

To Muslims the Koran is the Very Speech of God, revealed word for word to His Prophet Muḥammad through the angel Gabriel. For them there can be no question of earlier and later styles, phraseology, or doctrine; but the western student, recognizing in it the handiwork of Muḥammad the man, finds much of its interest in the way it reveals the gradual development of a fascinating personality and the stages by which his early teaching expanded into a new religion.

In the earliest portions of the Koran the reader has the feeling that Muḥammad is struggling with the means to express his ideas. He was not a practised speaker, and he had to create his own medium for the new message he felt impelled to deliver. The gift of words came with practice, but to the end the Koran expresses its theological and philosophic concepts in terms of symbolic action or description. Almost equally difficult was the problem of style. The High Arabic of the poets supplied an established linguistic medium, which had already been adapted to the practice of oratory; in rhetorical style, however, the concision sought by the poets was replaced by a looser and more expansive discourse, a habit of balancing phrase with phrase and of giving emphasis by parallelism in structure, assonance, and especially end-rhyme (*saj'*). Alongside this there continued to exist the traditional oracular style affected by the diviners, consisting of a series of obscure rhyming oaths (usually relating to celestial phenomena), followed by two or three brief rhymed phrases, often as obscure. It would seem that this oracular style had been adopted by the revivalist preachers at the Arab fairs, and since it had become, so to speak, the conventional style of religious discourse, Muḥammad had no alternative at the outset but to adopt it also. The earliest passages of the Koran are, accordingly, brief, semi-lyrical exhortations and warnings of the coming Judgement, often of great power and beauty:

When the sky is split and the stars are scattered,
When the seas are loosed and the graves are exposed,
A soul shall know what it has wrought in advance and what left behind.

Controversy in turn drove him to employ the allusive techniques of poetic satire, pointed, however, by sharp thrusts in the current Meccan idiom:

Perish the calculators
Who, sunk in an abyss of heedlessness,
Question, 'When, pray, the Day of Judgment?'
The day when [like base metal] they shall be tried upon the Fire!
Now savour your smelting—this is [the reckoning] you were so eager for!'

His Meccan opponents naturally classed him with the poets and soothsayers, who in the common belief were inspired by genii (*jinn*). The necessity of dispelling this belief, together with his growing command of language, led him by degrees to adopt a less lyrical style. The changing matter of the revelations led in the same direction, as they passed into narratives relating to former prophets and the fate of their opponents, arguments for the Resurrection from nature, and finally, in the Madīna period, to topical addresses and legal prescriptions. As the content of the Koran evolved, the linguistic structure evolved with it, to break away more and more from the conventional forms of aesthetic production of its time and to achieve a new, distinctive, and highly personal art. Form is subordinated to the presentation of the message, and in forcing the High Arabic idiom into the expression of new ranges of thought the Koran develops a bold and strikingly effective rhetorical prose in which all the resources of syntactical modulation are exploited with great freedom and originality.

As a literary monument the Koran thus stands by itself, a production unique in Arabic literature, having neither forerunners nor successors in its own idiom. Muslims of all ages are united in proclaiming the inimitability not only of its contents but of its style. But, as in the case of the old poetry, the very qualities which give it its literary distinction render it impossible to translate with any success into another language, and Islamic orthodoxy wisely discountenances any attempt to do so. The vigour and intensity of its language becomes vapid, the grammatical forms lose their subtle implications, the arresting rhetorical constructions become shapeless, and little is left but a seemingly confused and repetitious compilation, loosely strung together without life or artistry, and redeemed only by occasional flashes of mystical beauty or profound insight.

The influence of the Koran on the development of Arabic literature has been incalculable, and exerted in many directions. Its ideas, its language, its rhythms pervade all subsequent literary works in greater or lesser measure. Its specific linguistic features were not emulated, either in the chancery prose of the next century or in later prose writings, but it was at least partly due to the flexibility imparted by the Koran to the High Arabic idiom that the former could be so rapidly developed and adjusted to the new needs of imperial government and an expanding society. Even greater was its indirect influence, in that it was to the studies connected with the Koran that the majority of branches of Arabic literature owe their origin. Moreover, though the standard of literary Arabic was in fact set not by the Koran but by the heathen poets, it was due to the position of the Koran as 'Bible, Prayer-book, delectus, and first law-book to Muslims of whatever sect' that Arabic became a world-language and the common literary medium of all Muslim peoples. For the greater part of the period comprised in this chapter the work of studying the sacred text and of collecting the materials to assist in its elucidation went steadily forward, not itself leaving much mark on Arabic literature, but laying the foundation for the apparently sudden outburst that marks the early years of the next period.

Before tracing this development it is necessary to explain briefly the historical circumstances that contributed to it. Under Muḥammad's successors the Arabs, possessing for the first time a common rallying-cry and a central organization to direct their movements, swept out of Arabia into Syria and Iraq and shattered, with the aid of his disaffected subjects, the armies of the Emperor Heraclius and the exhausted power of Sasanid Persia. Thence in a series of rapid bounds they conquered Egypt, eastern Persia, the north African littoral, and within a century were masters of an empire extending from the Pyrenees to the Pamir. The organization of the new empire lies outside our scope, but the resulting redistribution of forces is of great importance for the history of Muslim religion and literature. The early theocratic organization of Madīna proved insufficient for the government of so vast a territory, and after its breakdown the civil capital of the Empire was transferred to Damascus, under the rule of the Umayyad dynasty, a Meccan family akin to the Prophet but imbued with political conceptions which squared ill with the views of the theocratic party. Madīna, however, remained the centre of religious learning, and it was there that the foundations of the 'Muslim sciences' (i.e. those connected with the study of the Koran) were laid. Mecca, on the other hand, enriched by the conquests and by its widening importance as the city of pilgrimage, rapidly developed habits of luxury and pleasure-seeking which were a scandal to the faithful. Central Arabia suffered the most striking change of all. Its most vigorous elements had joined the Muslim armies and returned to Arabia no more. The greater part of them settled in Mesopotamia and thence spread eastwards; smaller parties were scattered from Egypt as far as Spain. While they retained for the most part their nomadic habits, many of them eventually adopted settled life in the cities and on the land. There is no cause for surprise, therefore, that the true successors of the ancient poets almost all hail from Mesopotamia and rarely indeed from Arabia.

But the most vital result of the Arab conquests was the gradual absorption of the conquered peoples into the Islamic community. With them they brought the experience and habits of their distinctive civilizations and thus carried Arabic literature and thought to a stage of development beyond the unaided powers of the Arabs. It was not, however, until the close of our present period that their influence began to be felt. With few exceptions the studies which were carried on during the first century of the

Muslim era were carried on by Arabs, though it was partly the influx of such numbers of non-Arabic-speaking peoples into the Muslim community that led to the first steps in the development of the 'Muslim sciences'.

At the time when the Sacred Book was compiled, Arabic was written in a very imperfect script which was all but unreadable to those who did not possess an exhaustive knowledge of the language. It became a matter of urgency to preserve the text from corruption by establishing firstly a more adequate script, and in the second place the rules of Arabic grammar. As this need was most felt in the former Persian provinces the first attempts to meet it were made in the garrison cities of Iraq. The interpretation of the Koran also demanded careful study of its grammatical structure and vocabulary. Exact shades of meaning were defined by reference to the pre-Islamic poets, necessitating the collection and memorizing of their works. In this way arose the twin sciences of philology and lexicography, which were in consequence really based not on the Koran itself but on the ancient poetry. The application of Koranic passages was fixed by recollections of actions or sayings of the Prophet which had some bearing on the subject or the text. Rules for the conduct of life and affairs were also sought in the practice of the Prophet, and thus there came into being the most characteristic of Muslim literary activities, the science of Tradition. The study of the Koran and the Tradition supplied the basis upon which Theology and Jurisprudence, the obverse and reverse of the Sacred Law, were built. Though Madīna was still the centre of these studies, there is abundant evidence that they were pursued also in circles which were less sealed to foreign influences, both in Syria and in Iraq.

Two branches of the Muslim sciences further converged to lay the foundations of a study which soon overstepped their limits, that of History. On the one hand, philological studies entailed some researches into the history of pre-Islamic Arabia, as well as into the genealogies of the tribes. The demand produced the supply; narratives professing to relate the 'origins' and early history of the Arabs were concocted out of legends and vague traditions, probably filled out by borrowings from Judaeo-Christian sources and by pure invention. Several of these works, compiled by Arabs from Yemen, enjoyed great popularity in secular circles, especially at the court. On the other hand, the Tradition necessarily included much historical matter, chiefly in connexion with the Prophet's military expeditions (*maghāzī*). In spite of the opposition of some religious circles many students began to make a separate study of these historical traditions, and before the close of this period the first works on the subject were already in circulation. By their nature these works were more authentic than the old legends, and it was out of them that the later science of History was evolved.

The literary remains of all this activity are negligible, chiefly because at this stage the habit of oral transmission was still dominant, and perhaps even reinforced by religious discouragement of putting anything on paper except the Koran. The prejudice was most effective in the sphere of religious studies, which were, of course, those most pursued. Nevertheless, small private collections of traditions and poems were formed, and one at least of the former is still extant. The written historical or pseudo-historical works naturally passed out of circulation after their contents had been incorporated in later works. Over and above all this, prose as a literary medium was still in its infancy, practically confined, indeed, to chancery documents and rescripts, while writing materials of parchment, papyrus, or leather were precious and expensive. It was only in the next century, as we shall see, that after intense experimentation in different fields Arabic was endowed with a natural, comprehensive, and flexible prose style, just in time to take advantage of the discovery of the secret of paper manufacture.

Turning now to the poetry of this period, we find a very different situation. The rise of Islam reacted unfavourably at first on the old poetry. Muḥammad himself, although he had his court poet, Ḥassān ibn Thābit (upon whom, in consequence, much mediocre verse was fathered by later partisans), inevitably adopted a hostile attitude to it, as the chief moral force behind the pagan ideals which Islam had come to destroy. The early Muslim community and the theologians maintained this attitude after him. From this arises the astonishing fact that the birth and expansion of Islam inspired no poet in that nation of poets, and that the description of the Islamic movement in the grand manner of the ancient verse is limited to a single *ode by Kaʿb, the son of that Zuhair mentioned above as one of the chief didactic poets. Even the great poets already active in Arabia were reduced to silence; *Labīd, who combines in his work the expression of all that was best in the old Arabian life and who is represented in the *Muʿallaqāt*, lived more than thirty years into the era of the Hijra, but ceased to compose after his adhesion to Islam.

Before long, however, an impulse so ingrained was bound to reassert itself. It was no longer in Arabia, but in Mesopotamia, that the ancient tradition revived, with a new vigour and plasticity imparted to it by the political and social consequences of the Islamic movement. Externally there seems but little change; but although the Umayyad poets maintain the old conventions and canons of linguistic artistry, their productions reflect, for better or worse, the transformations resulting from the Arab conquests, the growth of luxury and a money economy, the rise of an imperial government and the imposition of its authority over the resentful and rebellious tribesmen, the emergence of religious and political parties and of organized tribal factions. Inevitably so, for the poets were still the mouthpieces of tribal and party sentiment. In the new situation they could achieve their functional purposes only if the purely formal qualities of their verse were overlaid to the extent that style and content complemented and harmonized with one another.

These changes are most clearly perceptible in the occasional poem, where old themes or types are adapted by individuals or schools to new purposes. New themes and new types of poetry emerge, the most remarkable being the independent love-poem to be described shortly. Eventually, after its brief eclipse, the *qaṣīda* too revived, and in its turn bears witness to the changing interests and values of the tribesmen, the more so that, like their predecessors, the *qaṣīd*-poets were of bedouin extraction. Towards the end of the seventh century there emerged a trio who rank among the masters of their art. Al-Akhṭal, of the Christian tribe of Taghlib in northern Mesopotamia, and the authentic continuator of the schools of an-Nābigha and ʿAmr ibn Kulthūm, stands closest to the spirit of pre-Islamic poetry, both in his tribal odes and his panegyrics of the Umayyad caliphs. The two others, *al-Farazdaq and Jarīr, were the idols of the tribesmen of Kūfa and Baṣra, and owed much of their fame to the entertainment they provided by slanging-matches on parallel themes (*naqā'iḍ*), a theatrical display of ingenuity and virtuosity, apart from a somewhat monotonous repertoire of personal taunts and indecencies. The very fact that major poets should so pander to the vulgar tastes of the urbanized tribesmen, however, shows how far they had departed from the simple, if narrow, loyalties and moralities of the old poetry. The passions of the Umayyad age were multiple and conflicting, and the poets shared in the general psychological instability and conflict of principles and parties. A copious sprinkling of Koranic phraseology and pious sentiment does not compensate for the coarser and shriller tones of their verse; and when they exploit the *qaṣīda* as an instrument to gain riches from the powerful and the wealthy, their adulation, more often than not blatantly hypocritical, is no longer phrased in terms of tribal virtues but of political and religious controversy.

The plain fact was that, although the *qaṣīda* remained the touchstone of poetical art, the themes of pre-Islamic poetry were becoming increasingly irrelevant to the new situation and environment of the Arabs. This was to some extent, perhaps even to a great extent, concealed by the nostalgia of the diaspora for the old free life of the desert, so that the evocation of deserted encampments and of desert journeys and hunting parties still inherited an emotional spell. Yet nothing could prevent these and like themes from becoming more and more formalized. It was not until the next period, however, that the *qaṣīda* was to freeze into an artificial convention, a self-conscious archaism, a mosaic of expressions and images derived from the ancient bards, to which, nevertheless, the poets remained bound by the pressures of tradition and the demands of their patrons.

In sharp contrast to all this is the new love-lyric, the *ghazal*, which suddenly appears in the now wealthy and luxurious cities of Mecca and Madīna. It is possible that the inspiration came originally from the Persian and Greek singers who gathered there in the service of the aristocracy of the Quraish. In the *ghazal* the sonorous vocabulary and artifices of the *qaṣīd*-poets are discarded for a simple, almost conversational style, and the traditional metres are slightly adapted, the better to meet the needs of singing. Its most brilliant exponent and the most remarkable of all the poets of the Umayyad age was the Quraishite *'Omar ibn Abī Rabī'a (d. *c.* 720). His poems, which breathe a tenderness as far removed from the primitive passion of Imru 'ul-Qais as from the hothouse sentiment of a later age, can perhaps be better compared with those of Herrick rather than Byron. The austere were scandalized, and the poet paid for his temerity by more than one exile, but contemporaries and later generations alike were haunted by the joyous youth, the freshness and chivalry of 'Omar's verse.

Ah for the throes of a heart sorely wounded!
Ah for the eyes that have smit me with madness!
Gently she moved in the calmness of beauty,
Moved as the bough to the light breeze of morning.
Dazzled my eyes as they gazed, till before me
All was a mist and confusion of figures.
Ne'er had I sought her, and ne'er had she sought me;
Fated the hour, and the love, and the meeting.[1]

In contrast to the *ghazals* of 'Omar and the other Meccan poets, realistic, urbane, and gay, the Madinian

[1] Translated by W. G. Palgrave in *Essays on Eastern Questions*.

ghazal depicts an idealizing, languishing, and hopeless love, with bedouin protagonists. Its apparent creator was Jamīl (d. 701), from whose tribe of 'Udhra this variety of *ghazal* was called 'Udhrite. From the moment of its creation, it achieved a great and growing popularity; Jamīl was followed by a host of 'martyrs of love', real or fictitious, whose woes and tears were destined to furnish themes to poets and romancers in Arabic, Persian, and Turkish for a thousand years. There is little to show that this was a genuinely bedouin art; on the contrary, such stories as that of Majnūn and Lailā, the self-immolating 'demented one' and his ever-inaccessible inamorata, seem rather to have flourished on the romantic nostalgia of the detribalized urban populations, especially in Iraq.

The influence of the Madinian *ghazal* is clearly visible in the later Iraqi poetry of this period, particularly in the art of Dhu'r-Rumma, surnamed 'the last of the poets' (d. 735), which is devoted mainly to descriptions of desert scenery and life, emotionalized by a *ghazal* theme. The Meccan *ghazal*, on the other hand, seems to have found admirers and imitators rather in Syria, where it encountered a native tradition of wine-songs. We know only the end-product of this confrontation, in the poetry and wine-songs of the Umayyad caliph Walīd II, whose profligate life, cut short in 744 by a revolt, paved the way for the downfall of his dynasty and the opening of a new era alike in Muslim history and Arabic literature.

5

THE GOLDEN AGE

(A.D. 750–1055)

THE new dynasty which assumed the headship of the Muhammadan world in 750, the 'Abbāsids, owed their elevation to alliance with the theocratic and legitimist parties among the Arabs and the support of the Persians and other subject-peoples. Self-interest, if nothing else, urged them to patronize the theological sciences and at the same time to encourage the talents of their Persian and Aramaean subjects. For three centuries this remained the constant tradition of the Caliphate and its provincial courts, as well as of the local Persian and Arab dynasties who supplanted the latter. The new capital Baghdād became the centre of literature and the arts, 'the market', as an Arab historian puts it, 'to which the wares of the sciences and arts were brought, where wisdom was sought as a man seeks after his stray camels, and whose judgement of values was accepted by the whole world'. The simultaneous outburst of literary activity had, as we have seen, its roots in the preceding period. By their unification of the Empire in government and language, and the consequent extension of the Muhammadan religion among their subjects, the Umayyads created the material conditions of which their successors reaped the advantage. The material which the humanist revival was to use was already being systematized; the new culture was already burgeoning, but the ʿAbbāsids by their tolerance and patronage gave it fuller scope and largely contributed to its splendour.

From this point the former subject-peoples take their place in every department of life and literature alongside the Arabs, each bringing the distinctive features of their culture to enrich the whole. From the time of Alexander all the civilized lands of the Near East had been profoundly influenced by Hellenism. Out of the resulting action and reaction arose a distinctively eastern branch of Hellenistic thought, which found expression in Alexandrian philosophy and the eastern Christian schisms. From the fourth century the Greek philosophers and their Neoplatonic commentators, the Greek astronomers, physicians, and scientists, were translated into Syriac and studied in the schools and monasteries of Syria and Mesopotamia. There still existed also a pagan community in northern Mesopotamia, who, under the name of 'Sabians', rendered great services to Muslim literature and science. In Egypt the Alexandrian schools of philosophy, medicine, and astronomy, though sadly diminished, remained sufficiently active to influence the work of the Muslims in the two latter sciences. This Hellenistic atmosphere also favoured the propagation of the Gnostic cults, a wide variety of eclectic systems strongly tinged with dualistic and Pythagorean teachings.

These were the contributions of the Aramaic and Hellenized peoples to Muslim literature and thought. Far less important was the material contribution of the Persians. The Sasanid Empire, cut off from the mainstream of Hellenistic culture, had little indigenous culture to put in its place. It is true that in later times a movement of literary nationalism in Persia sought to magnify the old Persian civilization at the expense of the Arabs, and to claim for Persia the origin of nearly everything of value in Muslim culture. But Persia under the Sasanids seems to have had little leisure or aptitude for literary pursuits, and what there was, if we may judge by its scanty survivals, was chiefly of a religious or legal sort, together with legendary stories of the ancient days and the exploits of the dynasty. In the neighbourhood of the capital, however, Hellenistic influences, spread by the Nestorians, had led to the founding of a school at Jundī-Shābūr, where the main subjects of study were again Greek philosophy and science, taught mainly by Nestorians. Alongside these, Indian philosophical and scientific works were translated and studied, and certain Iranian elements, both Mazdean and Manichaean, combined with the rest to form a peculiar syncretistic philosophy. The influence of this school was naturally strongest in Iraq, where it, with the earlier Gnostic syncretisms, was in a most favourable position to affect Islamic studies. Stronger Indian influences were introduced into the Muslim world by another Iranian community, of more mixed descent, which had been in prolonged contact with Buddhism in Bactria and Sogdiana. The view still expressed from time to time that the richer developments of Muslim culture and religious thought or of Arabic literature were due to the Iranians and represent aspects of an 'Aryan reaction against Semitic ideas' is an over-generalization from certain special cases. In Persia even at that time there could be as little question of racial purity as of a specifically 'Aryan' culture.[1] Except for the secretarial translations of Sasanid court-literature for the expanding bureaucracy, her main contributions were not literary, scientific, or philosophical, but the artistic temperament and natural

[1] Cf. L. Massignon, *Lexique de la Mystique musulmane*, p. 46.

genius and power of assimilation of her people, that found their finest expression under the stimulus of Islam.

It will now be plain why, with the change of dynasty, Arabic literature suddenly reached its Golden Age. Hitherto Muslim learning had been built up entirely by Arabs on an original plan, with at most indirect influence from the older centres of culture. In the burgeoning civic societies of Iraq it not only came face to face with foreign systems of thought, but, what was even more important, began to be studied by men whose whole mental outlook had for generations been moulded by Hellenism in one or other of its oriental offshoots. The immediate result was not unlike that produced by the reintroduction of Greek literature into Europe at the Renaissance. The two streams did not at once come into conflict. As we shall see later, the Muslim sciences themselves were more or less profoundly influenced by the Hellenistic tradition in method, outlook, and expression. The most effective legacies of Greek thought to the Islamic world were not, after all, in the sciences, but in method, order, and intellectual curiosity. Method and order came from the cultivation of logic (especially through the *Isagoge* of Porphyrius and Aristotle's *Organon*), and affected all branches of learning, from grammar and theology to geography and belles-lettres. But the most exciting quality of Muslim intellectual life in its third and fourth centuries is its curiosity, its desire to find explanations of everything, to learn about other countries and their ways, to study the stars and the nature of the human mind. This was the reason for the cultivation of the Greek sciences—experimental medicine, physics, music, mathematics—in all of which considerable advances were made and passed on to the awakening mind of Europe. Since, however, the Muslims did not draw directly on Greek sources (as Europe was to do at the Renaissance) but received them almost wholly at second hand through the medium of Syriac translations, they never came into contact with Greek literature as a whole, and remained ignorant of its intellectual and aesthetic qualities in poetry, drama, and belles-lettres.

It may, of course, be doubted whether, since the Arabs already possessed a highly developed poetry with its own criteria of aesthetic excellence, they would have understood or appreciated these qualities had they gained a fuller knowledge of Greek literature in its original tongue; it is enough to note that the opportunity was denied them. While the scholars cared only for its material content of fact and theory, however, the broader legacy of Hellenism, in conjunction with the Persian traditions, both stimulated and chimed in with the secular tone that pervaded Iraqi society in these centuries, a society bustling, worldly-wise, business-minded and somewhat cynical, but full of ideas. All this is reflected in the literature of the period, as scholars and students from Arabia, Syria, Egypt, and Persia found a new freedom of circulation. From their interaction in Baghdād and other centres of learning sprang a new Arabic literature that mirrored all its many-sided interests, and every development of which was carried rapidly to all corners of the Muslim world, from Samarqand to Spain.

The period covered in this chapter falls naturally into three divisions. The first, up to and including the reign of Hārūn ar-Rashīd (d. 809), covers the beginnings of a new Arabic prose literature. In the next 140 years, under the competing influences at Baghdād of Hellenism and the orthodox reaction, it bursts into full flower in all fields of intellectual and artistic endeavours. In the following century of political decentralization, it spreads from end to end of the Muslim world to create new and vigorous local centres.

§ 1. FROM A.D. 750 TO 813

It was natural that, apart from poetry, the branches of literature which first came into prominence were those closely connected with the studies and activities pursued in the Umayyad period. What most sharply distinguishes the new production, in both poetry and prose, is that it was, with few exceptions, produced by and for an urban society, concentrated mainly in Iraq, and that the majority of its producers were half-Arabs or non-Arabs, converts or descendants of converts from the original Aramaean and Persian population. Of the changes and developments that resulted from these new conditions the most significant is the emergence of an Arabic literary prose, clear, precise, and well-articulated. This was the final product of a confluence of literary activities, which, during this first ʿAbbāsid period, were pursued separately by the secretaries, the philologists, and the lawyers and Traditionists, and which we must now follow up respectively.

Under the last Umayyads the bureaucracy had begun to be reconstituted, largely from the same social classes that furnished the bureaucracy of the Persian Sasanid régime. The earliest Arabic prose works known to us are, in fact, three 'Epistles' composed by ʿAbd al-Ḥamīd b. Yaḥyā (d. 750), the secretary of the last Umayyad, Marwān II. It was, however, his Persian disciple Ruzbih, known as Ibn al-Muqaffaʿ (d. 757), who initiated the 'secretarial' school of letters by his extensive translations and adaptations of the Sasanian court-literature, including a version of the Persian hero-saga and 'Book of Kings' (both now lost) and of the famous Indian fables of Bidpai, under the title of *Kalīla and Dimna*. In their extant forms the surviving works of Ibn al-Muqaffaʿ have probably undergone some rehandling in later decades, but it is clear that he posed the problem of finding a smooth and palatable prose style, even at the cost of a breach with accepted Arabic tradition. The function of this secretarial literature was didactic and ceremonial. It laid down rules of conduct for princes, court officers, secretaries, and administrators of all kinds, and supplied the professional knowledge required for the performance of their duties, in the form of manuals, anecdotes, and romances. All this was comprised under the general head of 'manners' (*adab*), the secretarial tradition as a whole being founded on the doctrine that 'manners maketh man'. Because of their simple literary style and entertaining contents, these works gained wide popularity in the new urban society. When, about the year 800, the manufacture of paper in Baghdād provided ample supplies of cheap writing material, translations from and imitations of Persian romances multiplied right and left, and for some decades had the field almost to themselves, until the Arabic school began to compete with similar anecdotal collections and bedouin love-romances. Except for lists of titles, nothing whatever of them has survived.

The other two foci of literary production were the study of philology and the collection of Prophetic Tradition, neither of them as yet, however, narrowed down to a pedantic discipline, but rather the basis of a wide range of intellectual activities devoted to the Arabic language and to the Islamic heritage respectively.

Although Arabic philology undoubtedly arose out of the Koran, it has been clearly demonstrated that it was systematized, as it developed in Baṣra under the influence of the eclectic school of Jundī-Shābūr, on a totally different basis, the principal agent in which was the Aristotelian logic. The beginnings of the school of Baṣra are hidden in darkness. We hear vaguely of one or two names in the Umayyad period, but it is not until close on the turn of the century that we find definite historical figures. The first systematic expositions were made by al-Khalīl (d. 791), an Arab from Oman. On the basis of the ancient poetry he worked out a complex metrical theory which has never been superseded, and he made the first attempt to compile a dictionary, arranged not in any of the various alphabetic orders adopted in later Arabic lexicons, but according to a phonetic scheme in which Indian influences have been suspected. His pupil, the Persian Sībawaih (d. *c.* 793), rendered even greater services to Arabic philology. Working on the scattered researches of his predecessors, he combined the results into a systematic and logical exposition of Arabic grammar. His work (it is significant that it has never borne any title but *The Book), though improved at points by later writers, settled the principles of Arabic grammar once and for all, and still remains the standard authority.

Somewhat before this, but when and how is uncertain, a rival school of philology was set up at Kūfa (Najaf). Its teaching was marked by less emphasis on traditional forms, and represented, therefore, the modernist wing of philological science. The great authority of Sībawaih's Book won at a later period general acceptance for the views of the school of Baṣra, but for a time the two schools were engaged in a bitter academic rivalry. Both schools were at one, however, in setting themselves to counteract the degeneration and impoverishment of Arabic in the mixed society of the cities of Iraq, to define the correct modalities of High Arabic speech, and to preserve both the extensive vocabulary and the pure idiomatic usage of the peninsula. Thus, in opposition to the laxity of the secretaries, they reasserted in a new context the old Arabian insistence on the importance of form, thereby contributing to maintain the concept of High Arabic as a standardized and unchanging artistic structure, unaffected by the evolution and vagaries of spoken Arabic.

The method by which they pursued these ends, and again in conscious opposition to the secretarial school, was to search out and edit the old monuments of Arabic speech, the poems, proverbs, and tribal traditions of Arabia, in order to serve (in conjunction with the Koran and all the materials relating to the Islamic movement) as the basis of the 'Arabic humanities'. The grammarians of this early period were not dry schoolmen, but the humanists of Islam. Their work was inspired by practical aims. They had to meet the growing demand for education created by the bureaucratic organization of the Empire and the growth of an urban bourgeoisie, and the most famous scholars of the time were regularly entrusted with the education of the young princes. Their lecture courses were eagerly sought out, not only by young philologists and poets, but by men of letters of all kinds. Their discourses, compiled into monographs by their pupils, covered an immense variety of topics, both literary and historical. Of the two most famous scholars of Baṣra in the generation after al-Khalīl, al-Aṣmaʿī (d. *c.* 831) was preeminent in poetic criticism, and his rival Abū ʿObaida (d. *c.* 825), admiringly described by the poet Abū Nuwās as 'a skin stuffed with knowledge', in history. His exhaustive fund of detailed information on the histories of the tribes, both before and after the rise of Islam, was the main source from which later historians drew their materials.

But it was not only historians who exploited Abū ʿObaida's knowledge. Well before the end of this period the literary nationalist movement referred to earlier (p. 47) had been reinforced among the secretaries by rivalry with the philologists in their capacity of protagonists of the Arab tradition. The *Shuʿūbīya*, as the movement and its supporters were called, were mostly Persians by race or culture, and protagonists of the Sasanid tradition. They attacked the pretensions of the Arabs and their language, derided their poetry, and claimed not only equality but even superiority for the Persians and other non-Arabs in almost every department of life. The conflict continued through the next century, and is reflected not only in much of Iraqi literature, but even in theological and legal works. By no means all Persians were Shuʿūbīs; indeed, the defenders of the Arabs counted in their ranks almost as many Persians as their opponents. But for their exposure of the less creditable and even barbarous features of Arab tribal society, the Shuʿūbīs found chapter and verse in many of Abū ʿObaida's monographs, to such an extent that later generations regarded Abū ʿObaida himself (who was probably of Mesopotamian Jewish origin) as one of the most fanatical leaders of the *Shuʿūbīya*. Yet it was this same Abū ʿObaida who produced the first collected work on the exegesis of the Koran.

The main current of the second branch of studies, that of the Tradition of the Prophet, did not itself come into full literary activity during this period, but is represented by a few related disciplines. The most important of these was the study of Law. The orthodox standpoint of the

ʿAbbāsids made it imperative that the administration of the Empire should be brought (outwardly at least) into conformity with the principles of the Sacred Law as interpreted by the religious scholars, instead of following the somewhat arbitrary legal methods of the Umayyads. Before the death of Hārūn three of the still existing schools of law had already come into being. In the process of developing and expounding their bases and methodology (the extensive literature of which may well be omitted in this sketch) three works, one of each school, stand out as possessed of a wider importance. The dissatisfaction of the more conservative scholars with the speculative and foreign elements admitted by the school of Iraq was expressed by the Madīna doctor Mālik ibn Anas (d. 795). Placing the greatest weight on the traditions, not only of the Prophet but of the community at Madīna, whose common law might be regarded as the common law of the Prophet, Mālik compiled the traditions on which he himself, as a practising judge, based his decisions into a volume famous throughout the Muslim world under the title of *al-Muwaṭṭa'* ('The Levelled Path'). The second work is the masterly compilation known as **The Book of the Land-Tax*, made for Hārūn by his chief qadi, Abū Yūsuf (of the Iraqi or Ḥanafi school). Notwithstanding its title the work covers the whole range of practical administration from water-rights to the art of war, and is an indispensable commentary for every student of early Muslim history. The third is the 'Treatise' (*ar-Risāla*) in which the founder of the third school, ash-Shāfiʿī (d. 820), after lengthy argument with the leaders of the schools of both Madīna and Iraq, formulated the principles upon which all systems of Islamic Law were to be based henceforward, and more especially defined the exact limits and functions of the Prophetic Tradition in relation to the Koran. Quite apart from their significance in the general history of Islamic culture, the legal expositions and controversies illustrated by these three works were important in laying the foundations of a discursive and argumentative prose, which enabled the next generations to tackle with a reasonable degree of precision and flexibility the formidable task of rendering Greek philosophical texts and discussions into an adequate Arabic structure.

It was at this period also that the study of history was definitely established as an independent branch of the science of Tradition. On the basis of the earlier collections relating to the *maghāzī* (p. 40), Muḥammad *Ibn Isḥāq (d. 768), the grandson of a Mesopotamian convert, compiled the first full-scale 'Biography of the Prophet'. In its original state, in fact, it was much too full; it began with a history of the earlier prophets, based on the south-Arabian legends and Jewish sources, and only after this concentrated on the traditions relating to Muḥammad's life and mission in Mecca and Madīna. For the most part, the traditions on each event are cited singly and separately, with their transmitters and variations; but for the major events they are conflated into a single narrative and consciously assimilated to the traditional style of the old 'Battle-Days', with profuse citation of poems and verses relating to the occasion. The whole project met with such opposition from the religious scholars at Madīna that Ibn Isḥāq was driven to take refuge first in Egypt and then in Iraq, where the Caliph himself provided him with the means to complete the work. Once published, however, and in spite of severe criticism of its author for including many worthless and forged traditions and poems, the book was established as a classic, and in the recension of the Egyptian compiler Ibn Hishām (d. *c.* 833) has remained ever since the principal authority for the life of Muḥammad.

In the next generation the scope of historical writing was appreciably widened by another scholar associated with the school of Madīna. Al-Wāqidī (d. 823) not only wrote a large work on the *maghāzī* of the Prophet but also collected a stupendous body of materials from both oral and written sources on the personalities and events of the first two centuries of Islam. And although al-Wāqidī too was criticized in various quarters for sweeping into his net a number of unreliable or tendentious reports, his collections, mostly put into shape by his successors, constitute the indispensable foundation for the history of the early caliphate.

Meanwhile, in Iraq as well, several collectors had begun to compile the traditions of the Arab tribes settled in Kūfa and Baṣra after the conquests. These continue to display the main characteristics of tribal tradition in the pre-Islamic age, concentrating on particular episodes with luxuriant detail and citations of poetry, and at the same time sharply reflect the intensity of the political struggles of their age. Though patently one-sided, and confused in detail and chronology, these materials carry clear evidence of the extent to which their collection was influenced by the methods of the Madīna school, in that every statement is carefully documented with the names of the original narrator and its transmitters. Their historical value is by no means negligible, especially for the vivid insight they give into the inner factors of the first century of Islamic history. One such tradition may be singled out for special mention, that of the great tribe of Tamīm, which was propagated by Saif ibn 'Omar (d. 796) in the form of an historical romance of the conquests based largely on poetical materials in the manner of the old 'Battle-Days'; this has largely come down to us in the great compilation of aṭ-Ṭabarī (p. 81), owing to the chance that the latter, being primarily a religious scholar, placed the reputation of Saif as a traditionist higher than that of al-Wāqidī. Those who applied themselves more rigorously to the science of history were aware of the need to sift all these materials by applying to them the techniques of criticism which were being developed by the students of the Prophetic Tradition. This task was accomplished (to anticipate briefly) by the Baṣran scholar al-Madā'inī (d. 840), who organized most of the collections of his predecessors, including those of Abū 'Obaida and al-Wāqidī, in some 230 monographs. His work gained such a reputation for trustworthiness that it became the principal source for the major compilations of the following period (in which form alone it has come down to us), and has also stood up to modern critical investigation with remarkable success.

It is worth while pausing for a moment to note the surprising fact that within 200 years from the rise of Islam the Muslim community had assembled this enormous archive of materials on its pre-history in Arabia, its genesis, and its subsequent development. Moreover, it had done this out of its own resources; there is not a trace to be seen in it of either Byzantine or Persian inspiration. No doubt the natural pride taken in the extensive conquests and the rivalries of the Arab tribes contributed to this historical consciousness, but the principal factors were religious. In the theological view history was the theatre of the divine plan for the government of mankind, and the early split between Sunnīs and Shīʿa forced upon the mind of the community the significance of the events which had led up to and followed from it. Up to the end of this period the political and religious strands remained interwoven. This too was of major importance since, although partisans remained unalterably partisan, what may be called the classical core of historical studies learned from the science of Tradition the elements of critical analysis, through which the native credulousness and romanticism of Arabian memories were schooled by a measure of empiricism and respect for critical standards. This was the foundation of later Arabic and Islamic historiography, and from this time onwards history widens out into a multitude of channels and becomes an inseparable part of Islamic culture in all its regions.

While the new structure of Arabic prose was being hammered out in secretarial and scholastic circles, the currents and changes in the social life of the age still continued to find their artistic expression in poetry. The confrontation of Islamic society by Persian and Aramaean culture stimulated, both by attraction and repulsion, a wide range of emotional attitudes and reactions, and all of these were freely expressed in verse. The period opens, for example, with the appearance of a school of minor poets in Baṣra (apparently inspired by Walīd II), whose witty, uninhibited, and often scandalous verses met with a delighted reception in the new secular and pleasure-loving society of Iraq, and were even, set to music, enjoyed in the private entertainments in the royal palace. The other themes of Umayyad poetry of course persisted, but new elements were gradually fused into them. One of the most successful inventions was the courtly *ghazal*, short poems on themes of chivalrous love, created by 'Abbās ibn al-Aḥnaf (d. *c.* 807). Among the major poets these changes are to some extent masked by the continued cultivation of the *qaṣīda*, which now, even more than in the Umayyad age, acquired a ceremonial function, especially when the poet's reward was, as not infrequently, proportioned to the length of his ode. Yet the *qaṣīda* too was affected in several ways. One, to its advantage, was the pursuit of smoothness and simplicity in language, but without sacrificing any of the precision and variety of the High Arabic idiom. Both panegyric and satire are handled with considerable diversity and originality. But in another direction the poetry of this century prefigures the decline of the true poetic art and the growth of artificiality, as the pursuit of wit led to a straining after verbal brilliance and originality in metaphor and simile. This was the 'new style', the embellishment of verse by tropes and antitheses and the ingenious exploitation of the resources of Arabic morphology, disapprovingly called by the philologists *al-badī'*, 'the novel and strange'. It is first exemplified, although only in a moderate degree, in the work of the blind poet Bashshār ibn Burd (d. 784), of Iranian extraction, and the first major Arabic poet of non-Arab origin. One of his most famous similes runs:

Meseemed that upon their heads the dust of battle lay,
And our swords a night of flaming stars that cleave the abyss.

The elaboration of the *qaṣīda* with *badī'* devices is generally ascribed to a poet of the next generation, Muslim ibn al-Walīd, who was in consequence highly esteemed by some critics and condemned by others as 'the first who corrupted poetry'. The patronage of the court, however, powerfully seconded by popular favour, brought the new style into open recognition, in spite of the adverse opinion of the philologists.

But this was still in the future. There is little trace of these artifices in the work of the poet who stands head and shoulders above all his contemporaries in this period. Abū Nuwās (d. *c.* 803), half-Persian by origin, and apprenticed in his youth to the Baṣra school of poets, has indeed few rivals in Arabic poetry for genius, versatility, elegance, and command of language. Witty, gay, cynical, and foul-mouthed by turns, he was at his happiest in his incomparable drinking-songs, in which he takes occasion to loose his shafts in many directions, and especially (since he proudly identified himself with the Yemenites) to rip the pretensions of the northern Arab tribes. Ingenious in panegyric, coarse in satire and *ghazal*, a linguistic virtuoso in the bedouin style of hunting-poem (the fashion for which he revived), he stands on the one hand as the last of the natural troubadours in the Arabian tradition. The last, however, because, on the other hand, he and his contemporaries exemplify a new development which was almost immediately to affect all High Arabic poetry. Hitherto the poets had learned their art exclusively by association with their predecessors. With the rise of the philological schools, particularly at Baṣra, they began to perfect their training by systematic instruction from the philologists. There was good enough reason for this, since both poets and philologists shared the conviction that poetry was the guarantor of the pure tradition of Arabic linguistic art, and the *qaṣīda* the highest proof of the poet's mastery of it. But its effect was to imbue the poets themselves with a more or less philological approach to their art and an acceptance of philological criteria of poetic merit, especially in the article of the unapproachable superiority of pre-Islamic poetry. To this, probably, more than to any other single cause is due the formalization of Arabic poetry in the following centuries, and, in conjunction with the artifices of the 'new style', to its degeneration in the hands of the less gifted to an almost mechanical reproduction of well-worn themes with a surface decoration of *badīʿ*.

Not all poets, of course, were affected by these factors. A contemporary of Abū Nuwās, the Arab Abu 'l-ʿAtāhiya (d. 826), dared to break with tradition entirely in his output of didactic and moral verse. In order to gain the widest possible hearing, he deliberately discarded all the poetic conventions and mannerisms, used only the simple language of the people, and even experimented with new metrical schemes. However inferior in artistic genius and technique to Abū Nuwās, he gained for himself a popular reputation as lasting as that of the dissolute favourite of the court, and may justly be called the father of Arabic religious poetry. His more violent breaches with poetic conventions found no imitators, but his successors are to be seen on the one hand in the street preachers of Baṣra and on the other in the popular poetry, which diverged more and more widely from the productions in the High Arabic tradition as these grew more stilted and artificial.

§ 2. FROM A.D. 813 TO 945

With the occupation of Baghdād by Hārūn's son al-Ma'mūn after four years of disastrous civil war, a new phase opens in the development of Arabic literature. Ma'mūn himself was the son of a Persian mother, spent much of his early life in Persia, and won the throne largely by the aid of Persian troops. Intellectually, however, his leanings were towards the eclectic school of thought represented by the academy of Jundī-Shābūr (p. 53). He encouraged the translation and study of Greek philosophical and scientific works by founding in Baghdād an academy, called *Bait al-Ḥikma* ('House of Wisdom'), and took a prominent part in religious and philosophical discussions. In this attitude he was followed by his first and second successors, and thus for quarter of a century Hellenistic influences found full liberty of expression throughout the Empire. No doubt, these studies in their stricter sense were pursued less by Arabs than by converts, who brought with them into Islamic circles the almost unquestioned acceptance of the truth of philosophy and the semi-religious prestige which had attached to it in all the eastern lands. But with increasing social interaction and expanding material and economic development, the diffused legacy of Hellenism among the educated classes of western Asia confronted the Arabic and Islamic traditions in almost all fields of intellectual culture. The Arabic literature of the next two and a half centuries, both religious and secular, is all but dominated by the attractions and repulsions resulting from their confrontation.

It would be out of place to review in this survey the technical literatures of science and philosophy, but the significance of the Hellenistic transmissions and the range of specialist disciplines which they introduced cannot be appreciated without some account of the leading figures. The earliest translator on a large scale was Quṣṭā ibn Lūqā of Baʿalbek (*fl.* 835), who not only made many renderings of Aristotle and many later writers but himself wrote copiously on mathematics, astronomy, and other subjects. His fame was eclipsed by Ḥunain b. Isḥāq (d. 873), the translator of Plato and Galen, who studied Greek in Anatolia and under the orthodox reaction supplanted the Christian family of Bukhtyashū' (which had held the post for several generations) as physician to the Caliph. The zeal of translators sometimes outran the bounds of discretion. Some of the *Enneads* of Plotinus appeared under the title of **The Theology of Aristotle*; the genuineness of the ascription was never questioned, and the work remained as a further element of confusion in the welter of philosophies which the Muslim strove to harmonize. The first student of the Greeks to make his name in Arabic philosophy was al-Kindī (d. *c.* 850), whose pure Arab descent earned him the title of 'the Philosopher of the Arabs'. He took the whole field of Greek science for his portion, and is credited with no fewer than 265 treatises on such various subjects as music, astronomy, mathematics, and medicine, as well as on ethics, logic, and metaphysics. In his ethics he reflects the late Hellenistic blending of Platonic, Peripatetic, and Stoic elements; in his surviving treatise on metaphysics he, like almost all Muslim philosophers, aims at reconciling Aristotle with Islamic teaching on the creation of the world. It is in this treatise that he makes his famous claim for the rights of rational investigation: 'It should be no shame to us to honour truth and make it our own, no matter whence it may come, even though from far distant races and peoples who differ from us.'

The chief name in the early history of Arabic mathematical science is *al-Khwārizmī (d. *c.* 844). With the encouragement of Ma'mūn, he studied not only the Greek works on mathematics and astronomy but also the Indian systems which had been translated into Arabic some years earlier. By the use of Indian numerals he revolutionized methods of reckoning, and it was from the Latin translations of his works on algebra and astronomy that Europe received the decimal notation ('Arabic numerals'), which were called by his name ('algorism') throughout the Middle Ages. Al-Khwārizmī also produced a revision of Ptolemy's *Geography* for al-Kindī. Equally famous in medieval times were the astronomical works of his contemporary al-Farghānī ('Alfraganus'), of Kindī's pupil Abū Maʿshar of Balkh ('Albumaser', d. 886), and of al-Battānī ('Albategnius', d. 929). In medicine the legacy of Galen was expanded by Ibn Māsawaih (d. 859), and above all by the greatest of the medieval doctors, ar-Rāzī (d. *c.* 930), known to Europe as Rhazes. Most of his life was spent in Persia, but he held for a time the post of physician-in-chief at the great hospital of Baghdād. A number of his treatises have come down to us, both in Arabic and in medieval Latin translations, including his great posthumous work called *al-Ḥāwī* ('Continens'), several compendiums, and numerous monographs including a celebrated one on small-pox. Among the most interesting features of his work are his clinical reports of cases, which formed a mine of material for later collectors of anecdotes.[1] In philosophy, too, he was a man of original mind whose sceptical attitude towards all religions aroused universal opposition and attack, with the natural consequence that only some *small segments of his philosophical writings have survived.

The first reactions to the Hellenistic revival came, as might be expected, in the field of theology. As the prevailing Hellenistic philosophy was Neoplatonic, it immediately became a matter of acute importance to define the

[1] An example will be found in E. G. Browne's *Arabian Medicine* (pp. 51–53), from which the above details have been taken.

relation between its philosophic pantheism and the rigid monotheism of the Koran. The first faint stirrings of the spirit of inquiry had been manifested among the Arabs as early as the first century of Islam. It was possibly as a result of Christian controversy in Syria that the movement first crystallized round a definite point, the reality of human freedom against the orthodox doctrine of predestination (*Qadar*). As foreign influences grew stronger the movement widened in scope, and became identified with the school called *al-Muʿtazila* (the 'seceders' or 'neutrals'), into which the Qadarite school was merged. The traditionists were suspicious from the first, but were not yet in a position to prevent or to control its manifestations. A cultivated society, reared on Aristotelian logic and full of admiration for the wonders of Greek science, inevitably accepted their premisses and was stirred thereby to an insatiable intellectual curiosity. Moreover, the early Muʿtazilites proved themselves to be zealous champions of Islam against the dualist heresies which still had a popular appeal in Iraq. So long as they were content to sustain this missionary role and to confine their theological discussions to a small academic circle, there seemed little to be feared from philosophical controversy.

The situation was radically altered when Ma'mūn publicly declared for the Muʿtazilite heresy and imposed an inquisition on the orthodox. Supported by the civil power, Muʿtazilism threw discretion to the winds and its leaders gave vent to theories each more revolutionary than the last.

They were applying to the ideas of the Koran the keen solvent of Greek dialectic, and the results which they obtained were of the most fantastically original character. Thrown into the wide sea and utter freedom of Greek thought, they had lost touch with the ground of ordinary life, with its reasonable probabilities, and were swinging loose on a wild hunt after ultimate truth, wielding as their weapons definitions and syllogisms.[1]

We are not concerned here with their names and their works; the orthodox saw to it that little or nothing of those survived, and their importance for Arabic literature lies in the influence they exerted and the opposition they stirred up. In proportion as Muʿtazilism became more daring in its assaults on orthodoxy, the defenders of the citadel became more tenacious in their defiance. Rejecting everything that savoured of the hated heresy, refusing even to admit discussion, they fell back on the Koran and the Tradition and met all questions with *Bilā kaif*, 'Don't ask "How?"'. Their champion, and the idol of the Baghdād mob, was Aḥmad b. Ḥanbal (d. 855), the foremost traditionist of his age.

With the accession of the Caliph al-Mutawakkil (847–61) the tide began to turn against the Muʿtazilites. Within a century of its foundation the ʿAbbāsid house had exhausted its vigour, and lived on at the mercy of its imported or self-appointed defenders. Like all Muslim dynasties it was only in its young and vigorous days that it gave unrestricted patronage to all students of science and literature; as it decayed it felt more strongly the need of conciliating the powerful influence wielded by the theologians. Their support was given only at a price, although as yet the spirit of inquiry and the latent genius that had broken through in the Muslim community were too powerful to be uprooted. Mutawakkil did what he could; he gave the support of the civil power to the orthodox; he silenced *al-Muḥāsibī, the most prominent Ṣūfī teacher

[1] D. B. Macdonald, *Development of Muslim Theology*, p. 140.

in Baghdād; he outlawed the Shīʿa and enforced drastic sumptuary and civil regulations against Christians and Jews. The mob seconded his efforts, and every poet or writer who showed the least sign of independence was liable to be lynched as a Muʿtazilite.

Muʿtazilism remained a menace, however, so long as the orthodox rejected every appeal to reason. The theologians could assure their victory only by learning from their opponents and using their own dialectic weapons against them. A new scholastic theology, reconciling Greek physics with the data of the Koran and the Tradition, was formulated simultaneously in Baghdād, Egypt, and Samarqand, and gradually argued Muʿtazilism out of existence. The chief credit for this was reaped by *al-Ashʿarī (d. 935), the leader of the movement in Baghdād, who had himself been educated in Muʿtazilite circles. The milder Muʿtazilites became the left wing of the scholastic theologians, and the more radical found a new sphere of activity in Shiʿism. The Ashʿarite school also had its trials, however; the Ḥanbalites still maintained their opposition to any discussion, and it took a century and a half before Ashʿarism established itself as the universal scholastic theology of Sunnī Islam.

Scarcely had the orthodox turned the tables on Muʿtazilism than they became aware of new dangers threatening them from a movement hitherto closely allied with them. From the earliest days of Islam many believers were noted for their ascetic practices. The discipline of these early devotees was to recite the Koran through over and over again, until the 'inner meaning' of each verse should become a living reality to them. The best type of first-century asceticism is al-Ḥasan of Baṣra (d. 728). To a life of singular devotion and courage he added a sound intellect and a fine gift of eloquence, displayed in the sermons which have been preserved to us. His memory, in spite of attacks by the literalist theologians of a later age, remains fragrant in Islam to this day. In the second century this simple asceticism became more vigorous and, while remaining wholly within the community, developed a number of distinctive practices. We hear of monastic retreats and of street 'preachers' at Baṣra and elsewhere. These ascetics (about this time the term *Ṣūfī* began to be applied to them) were found among the Qadarites and Shiʿites as well as among the orthodox. It was inevitable that the primitive Islamic mysticism should be affected by older currents of popular religion in western Asia, and more especially by various forms of Gnosticism. By the third century most of these accretions had been pruned away, and the elements that remained, even if not strictly Koranic, had been linked on to the Koran. The most conspicuous instance is the change-over from the ascetic motive of fear of God to the devotional and mystical motive of love of God, expressed most beautifully and simply by the poetess *Rābiʿa of Baṣra (d. 801). It is hard not to see in this the influence of Syriac mysticism.

So far the objects and methods of the Ṣūfīs involved nothing repugnant to the general sense of Islam. But when, in the third century, the mystical love of God developed into ecstasy expressed in symbolist images; when the esoteric sufistic interpretations of the Koran began to diverge more widely from its accepted outward sense, and the Ṣūfīs to claim freedom from the religious practices incumbent on all Muslims; when, to the horror of the uninitiate, Ṣūfīs were heard to speak of the Deity in the first person—the theologians realized that they must arm for another struggle. All this was as yet, perhaps, confined to a few advanced thinkers; it was not until the next century that the old-time meeting for recitation of the Koran (*dhikr*) became in certain circles a means to induce ecstasy by various methods of autohypnosis. The bulk of the Ṣūfīs were still at one with their fellow-Muslims in their beliefs and practices, and it was in Ṣūfī circles that the arguments of the Muʿtazilites were first countered by their own weapons. Nevertheless, the tendency of Ṣūfīsm was to widen the breach between theologian and mystic, and when its views were erected into a unified, if complex, rival doctrine, the theologians felt that it was time to strike. The chief figure in the struggle was the Persian *al-Ḥallāj, who represents the culmination of the early mystic movement. His life, doctrines, and extant writings have been exhaustively studied in a series of monographs by Professor Massignon, who has amply vindicated the fundamental orthodoxy of al-Ḥallāj against the speculative pantheism with which he was formerly charged. But his popularity alarmed the weak government of Baghdād, and on the ground of some incautious phrases he was condemned by a theological council and cruelly executed in 921. After his death Ṣūfīsm continued to develop along two lines: one which sought to reconcile the mystic life with orthodox (Ashʿarite) theology, the leading literary figure in which prior to Ghazālī (p. 120) is al-Qushairī (d. 1074), the author of a popular *treatise (*Risāla*); and another which diverged more and more into pantheism and antinomianism. Although the latter struck deeper roots in Persian than in Arabic soil, we shall meet with it later in Arabic literature.

It has been necessary to deal fully with these religious controversies for two reasons. The omission of all reference to theological literature would present a distorted picture of Arabic literature, of which the vast bulk is religious in scope. In the second place they supply the background for all the literature of the period, as nearly every writer of importance was concerned in one way or another with the disputes, and his attitude towards them is reflected in his works. It will not, however, be necessary for us to deal again with religious movements, except in connexion with those later writers who occupy a special position both in literature and theology.

The most important literary movement connected with the orthodox reaction was the definitive collection of the Tradition. Though Mālik ibn Anas (p. 56) and the orthodox theologians had established the principle that the law must be based on the traditions, the great body of traditionists studied them less from the legal than from the theological standpoint, and no traditionist was qualified for judicial office unless he had also studied jurisprudence. To remedy this a new method of presenting the Tradition was devised. The older compilations, of which the *Musnad* of Ibn Ḥanbal (p. 68) is the most important, had been aimed, at least partly, to shore up traditional Islam against the critical positions of the Muʿtazilites. In them, traditions were grouped without regard to their subject-matter under the name of that contemporary of Muḥammad who was cited as the original authority. In the new system they were arranged in order of subject-matter, with the aim of showing that the study of the Tradition provided in itself a practical legal training.

The first of the new collections, compiled by *al-Bukhārī (d. 870), although it includes traditions of all sorts, biographical, ethical, and medical, as well as purely legal, was intended to serve as a handbook of jurisprudence. Each section is headed by a statement explaining the legal application of the traditions it contains; in some cases even we find chapter-headings without appended traditions, thus betraying the subjective methods followed by its author. The contemporary collection made by Muslim (d. 875), on the other hand, leaves the application of each tradition to the reader and aims more at presenting a complete collection of all the 'sound' traditions.

It was more than time that such an attempt was made. The story of the development of the Tradition in Islam is a most curious one. As the problems of the early community became more complex it was usual in theological circles to deduce what the practice (*sunna*) of the Prophet would have been under each new set of circumstances, and pass their judgement into circulation as a tradition (*ḥadīth*) emanating from the Prophet himself. These judgements, swayed by the conflicting views of sects and parties, were naturally often in open contradiction. The students of Tradition, faced with the necessity of discriminating between them, fastened first on the authenticity of the chain of authorities (*isnād*) by which the tradition was supported. Every genuine tradition, it was held, must be guaranteed by some reliable person who himself had heard it from an earlier traditionist, and so on back to a contemporary of the Prophet who vouched for having heard the Prophet saying the words or seen him doing the action related therein. An *isnād* could as easily be forged as a tradition, however, and so, for two centuries, every movement in Islam endeavoured to gain support for its aims by putting into the mouth of the Prophet utterances in favour of its particular views. When the Shi'ites, for example, claimed the right of the house of 'Alī to the Caliphate, the orthodox countered with the tradition 'We

Prophets have no heirs'. When the ascetics put into Muḥammad's mouth injunctions to forsake the world, the busy lawyers and men of affairs replied by traditions enjoining due attention to worldly matters. The conflict spread even into history, where there is only too much reason to suspect that not only the presentation of major episodes but many seemingly minor details hide a polemical or pragmatic purpose behind a bland exterior.

In such circumstances it became imperative to establish a corpus of traditions which could be accepted as genuine. The traditionists, still holding (at least outwardly) to the *isnād* criterion, eventually came to a general agreement that only certain chains of transmission could be regarded as authoritative. It was on these principles that both Bukhārī and Muslim selected their traditions out of a mass of several hundred thousand, and gave the name *Ṣaḥīḥ* (Sound) to their collections. Their judgement was accepted, and the two *Ṣaḥīḥs* hold in all subsequent history of Islam a place second only to the Koran, not so much that they decided once and for all which traditions were genuine and which false, but because they brought together all that was already recognized as genuine in orthodox circles. These two works were subsequently supplemented by four others of the same period, with which they form the six 'canonical' works of Islamic tradition. The collection of traditions continued for several centuries, but few of the later compilations are of special importance in the history of Arabic literature. On the other hand, the books of Tradition, and especially that of Bukhārī, by their appeal to simple piety and veneration for the Prophet, proved to be one of the most potent forces in maintaining the spiritual vigour and solidarity of the Muslim community. For parallel reasons, the Shīʿites, too, although they accepted the two *Ṣaḥīḥs* in part, felt it imperative to produce their own standard collections of *ḥadīths* attributed to the ʿAlid Imāms, beginning with that of al-Kulīnī (d. 939).

To return now to the general field of secular literature and belles-lettres, the problem that remained to be solved at the beginning of the ninth century was how to bring the Arabic humanities out of their scholarly or technical isolation into a positive relation with the public interests and social issues of the day, and thus effectively challenge the pretensions of the secretarial school. The problem was illuminated, rather than solved, by ʿAmr b. Baḥr, known as al-Jāḥiẓ ('the goggle-eyed'), grandson of a negro slave, and the most genial writer of the age, if not of Arabic literature altogether. He died, more than ninety years old, in 869. Endowed with a remarkable power of assimilation, he forced his way up from very humble beginnings, studied philology in the school of his native Baṣra and theology under the celebrated Muʿtazilite teacher an-Naẓẓām, and took a keen interest in Greek philosophy and science. A man of his mould could not forego his independence; he resigned an official post three days after his appointment, and even in law he formed a school of his own. Although a Muʿtazilite, his views were so tempered by his breadth of mind that, we are told, 'he was held in high esteem among both Muʿtazilites and non-Muʿtazilites, by all the learned who knew men and could judge affairs', and even the fanatical Mutawakkil appointed him tutor to his sons. He writes with immense zest and vigour and a loquacity that seems to flow of its own accord out of a boundless reservoir of Arabic learning, alternately grave and gay, exalted and extravagant. His wit was ready and sometimes mordant, and his range universal. He was an indefatigable reader, and the story goes that he used to hire booksellers' shops so that he could sit up reading all night.

Of his works there have come down to us, apart from theological tracts and a large work on rhetoric, some thirty or forty *treatises and a collection of essays entitled *The Book of Animals*. The very titles of the former suggest his originality: 'The Boast of the Blacks over the Whites', 'The Merits of the Turks', 'In Praise of Merchants and Disparagement of Officials', 'The Superiority of Speech to Silence', &c. *The Book of Animals*, his masterpiece, fills seven volumes, in which zoology plays a minor part. After a long introduction including, amongst other matters, a section in praise of books and on the origins of writing, the first and second volumes are devoted to dogs. The material is cast loosely into the form of a debate between the 'Fowl-keeper' and the 'Dog-owner', and the bad and good qualities of dogs are illustrated by quotations from traditions, poems, proverbs, anecdotes, even extracts from the Koran. Popular superstitions are brought in—how the dog is reputed to be the horse of the Jinn, its place in the science of augury, and how the madness caused by its bite may be cured by the blood of kings and nobles. The remaining volumes treat more briefly but as discursively of the other animals and insects known to the ancient Arabs. In later days his methods were copied by many plagiarists, and we possess a work by one such pseudo-Jāḥiẓ, **The Book of Beauties and Antitheses*, on various physical and moral qualities.

Brilliant as the writing of al-Jāḥiẓ was, his style was too individual to serve as the model for general literature. The final solution was found by his later contemporaries, who blended the clarity of the secretarial style with the traditional art-language and the argumentative prose of the philological and legal schools into a medium capable of expressing all varieties of factual, imaginative, and abstract subjects with great refinement and precision. This was the new 'standard' Arabic which, at the cost of discarding something of the vigour and superfluous wealth of the ancient idiom dear to the philologists, served its purpose for a thousand years. The man who may be called the founder of the new school was Ibn Qutaiba of Merv (d. 889). In a long series of works he aimed to furnish the secretaries and the reading public with compendia and extracts from all branches of Arabic learning, but incorporated in them also those elements of the Persian historical and court-literature which could be harmonized with the Arabic and Islamic humanities.

His chief composition is a literary thesaurus, **The Fountains of Story*, in ten books. So many later works conform to its general plan that it may stand for us as the original type of the essay in Arabic literature. Each book deals with a given subject, sovereignty, war, friendship, asceticism, and the like, and under each heading and sub-heading are inserted quotations from the Tradition, the poets, and from literary and historical sources. The author allows himself certain liberties with his matter, abridging and freely revising to gain enhanced effect. In capable hands the result is both pleasing and interesting, though it must be confessed that the taste is an acquired one. Of smaller compass are his *Book of Subjects of Knowledge*, a summary of the early traditions of the Arabs and Persians together with very brief biographies of the chief figures in Islamic history, and *The Book of Poetry and Poets*. In the *introduction to this work, which contains short biographies of all the pre- and post-Islamic poets with illustrative examples of their poetry, he raises a voice, for the first time in Arabic philology, against the dogma of the matchlessness of the pre-Islamic poets:

I have not preferred the ancient poet for his antiquity nor scorned the modern poet for his recency, but have scanned both with an equitable eye and given each one his due. . . . God has not limited learning and poetry and eloquence to one age rather than another, nor distinguished one people thereby above another, but has made it a joint heritage among His servants in every age, and has made every ancient thing new in its time and every honour parvenu at its beginning.

As well as a manual of style for the use of the secretaries and a work on the reconciliation of divergent Traditions, he wrote a number of smaller treatises, the most interesting of which is a witty defence of the Arabs against the *Shuʿūbīya* (p. 55), and all the more effective in coming from the pen of a Persian.

Henceforward *adab*, in its literary sense, was no longer confined to the secretarial manuals of etiquette, but applied to all treatises based on this widened Arabic–Islamic tradition, including both the adaptations from Persian and Hellenistic sources. The mainstream of Arabic belles-lettres after Ibn Qutaiba runs through miscellaneous topics drawn from Arab poetry and history, politics and rhetoric, anthologies and collections of anecdotes, and popular ethics. The professional philologists supplemented the first by collections called *Majālis*, 'Sessions', or *Āmālī*, 'Dictations', but except for a few works of the next period, the more strictly scientific and philosophical works of the Greeks remained entirely marginal to *adab*. This may be partly explained by the phenomenon familiar to us in our own day, that the technical vocabulary of the sciences, as they developed, however well adjusted to their proper purposes, was unfamiliar and little understood outside the circles of specialists, but still more, probably, because these circles themselves remained somewhat apart from the general body of literary culture and pursuits.

It was very different with history, which, although properly distinct from *adab*, was to some extent affected by the same influences and became an essential part of the equipment of an educated man. In the first half of this century it was still predominantly associated with religious studies, and the most important new development was the working up of the materials collected by Wāqidī, Madā'inī, and others into finished works. At the same stage, historical composition breaks into two main divisions, biography and annalistic. Wāqidī's secretary Muḥammad Ibn Sa'd (d. 845) initiated the former with a vast biographical dictionary covering the first two generations of Muslims, prefaced by a two-volume biography of the Prophet, and was followed by a series of biographical 'histories' of various cities, devoted chiefly to their scholars and *qāḍīs*. The first of the group of notable historians of the age, al-Balādhurī (d. 892), also organized his major historical work, *The Genealogies of the Nobles*, on a biographical pattern, in which the history of the first century of Islam is presented within a framework of tribes and families. But his shorter **History of the Conquests* is purely annalistic; it gives a consecutive narrative of the conquest and subsequent history of each province separately, and generally omits variant traditions. About the same time, al-Ya'qūbī (d. after 891) wrote on similar lines a chronological summary of universal history from the Shi'ite point of view, as well as a work on *historical geography, the earliest of its kind in Arabic literature.

Valuable as both these works are, they are far outstripped by the vast history of aṭ-Ṭabarī (d. 923). It is characteristic of Muslim learning in the last few centuries that, while the great oriental libraries of the Middle Ages often contained as many as twenty copies of this work, it was left to a band of European scholars towards the end of last century to restore it to Arabic literature by piecing together a number of scattered manuscripts. Ṭabarī represents the humane learning of his age at its best. Born at Āmul in Ṭabaristan in 839, he studied at Rayy, just missed Ibn Ḥanbal at Baghdād, and subsequently heard various teachers at Baṣra, Kūfa, the towns of Syria, and Fusṭāṭ (Old Cairo), before settling in Baghdād. After forty years' study he had acquired all the theological, philological, and historical learning of early Islam in a completeness probably unequalled before or since. For forty years more he gave himself up to teaching and writing. He was essentially a traditionist, but independent withal; he founded a separate school of law (which barely survived him), and he set himself two great literary tasks.

The highest object of scientific study remained for him, of course, the Revelation, which, however, he regarded in a double aspect: as the written Word of God in the Koran, and as the manifestation of the Will of God in History. So there came into existence one after the other his Koran Commentary and his Universal History, the latter based likewise upon theological principles. In the following period both of these works formed the foundations of the Koranic and historical sciences. The history, which is unquestionably the weaker of the two and shows many defects in the composition (which are excused by the advanced age of the author), attained an authoritative position more speedily and fully than the former, because it had scarcely any competitors and its matter was not, like Koranic exegesis, the battlefield of contending parties. Yet by the unanimous judgement of all impartial men, there existed no earlier or later work which even approached

Ṭabarī's commentary in universality of material, positive knowledge, and independence of judgement, and in the eastern Muslim world orthodox scientific Koran study gradually submitted to his authority.[1]

His history, unlike the selective method of Balādhurī, gives a chronicle of events year by year, not in one continuous narrative but as related by his different authorities. His aim was to unite in one book all the historical traditions of the Arabs, both from the early tribal sources as well as the more critical work of Madā'inī, just as he had previously collected all the traditions relative to the Koran, but here for some reason he rarely criticizes or indicates any preference. The book thus presents an appearance of incoherence, and is deficient in some respects (the conquest of Spain, for instance, is dismissed in six lines), but it is noteworthy that only since the publication of Ṭabarī's history has it been possible to obtain a clear and trustworthy picture of the early history of Islam. For the *pre-Islamic period he follows the usual 'authorities' for Arabic and Persian history.

In vivid contrast is the method followed by Ṭabarī's successor al-Mas'ūdī (d. 956). He in his early life studied not theology but science and philosophy, and spent many years in travelling through the East both by land and sea. The insight and experience gained by contact with other peoples, together with his early studies and his Hellenistic curiosity about all things terrestrial and celestial, supplied the material for his elaborate encyclopaedia of the history, geography, philosophy, and religions of the Muslims, their neighbours, and predecessors. Unfortunately only one volume, and that the least valuable, of the thirty that made up his original work has come down to us, and only

[1] O. Loth in *Zeitsch. für Deutsche Morgenländ. Gesell.* xxxv. 589 ff.

one of his first abridgement. A second abridgement entitled **The Golden Meadows*, in some 600 pages, is all that we have to judge our loss by. There is no more delightful work in Arabic. The inconsequent style of the author as he ranges over natural history, history, geography, ethnology, religion, medicine, and what not, his breadth of view and innumerable anecdotes, keep the reader interested and amused; and though he almost always refers the curious to his larger works for detailed accounts, the summary preserves a good deal of valuable historical matter. Some years before his death he wrote, at Old Cairo, a brief analytic index, with addenda, to his former works under the title of **The Book of Indication and Revision.*

It is obvious from Yaʿqūbī's and Masʿūdī's works that by the end of the ninth century the concept of history had already emerged from its religious matrix and broadened out to constitute an independent science. The 'universal history', to be sure, is universal only in the limited sense that, beginning with the Creation, it offers a summary of world-history in larger or smaller compass by way of introduction to Islamic history proper, and from the moment of the rise of Islam shows little or no interest in the history of other communities. A more significant index of the growing interest in history for its own sake is furnished by such works as the *History of Baghdād* by Ṭaifūr (d. 893), of which one volume only has survived, the *History of the Viziers* by al-Jahshiyārī (d. 942), and, on somewhat different lines, the literary-historical *memoirs of aṣ-Ṣūlī (d. 946), which prelude the new developments of the next century.

About the same time an extensive and varied geographical literature came into existence. The needs of administration were responsible for the earliest Arabic geographical work. As in the classical age, the postal service of the Muslim Empire was organized purely as a department of government. It seems that the Arabs took over the Roman and Persian systems much as they stood and even preserved the old technical nomenclature. The centralizing tendencies of the ʿAbbāsids led them to pay special attention to the upkeep of the means of communication, and it was the postmaster at the new capital Sāmarrā, *Ibn Khurdādhbih, who in 844 compiled the first list of post-roads. Taking one province at a time, he gives lists of post-stations and the distances between each, and concludes with a summary of the revenues due from each district.

Other factors also combined to stimulate the expansion of geographical writing: the Hellenistic impulse, evidenced in the work of al-Khwārizmī (p. 66) and al-Masʿūdī, the older philological interest in the place-names of Arabia, and various concepts and materials derived from Persia and India. In no department of literature is the intellectual curiosity of the time, in both its finer and cruder aspects, more richly displayed: road-books on the lines of Ibn Khurdādhbih, scientific works on mathematical geography, books of maps and sailors' charts, descriptions of 'marvels' and curiosities, travellers' guide-books, all find a place. Valuable and interesting as they all are, we are most attracted by the work of the descriptive geographers. Yaʿqūbī has already been mentioned; in the tenth century he was followed by a series of indefatigable travellers, who between them traversed the Muslim world from end to end and have left us detailed accounts of the different provinces from personal observation. The two greatest were Ibn Ḥawqal, who in 977 expanded an earlier work written by *al-Iṣṭakhrī in 951, and *al-Maqdisī, whose book was first published in 985 and revised in 988. Both were animated by a passion for accuracy; Maqdisī, however, not only excels Ibn Ḥawqal in literary craftsmanship, but even to some extent anticipated our modern organic geography by extending his survey to the different manners, customs, beliefs, and good and bad qualities of the peoples whose lands he visited.

We possess also a number of very interesting accounts of embassies to foreign lands, such as that sent into Russia under *Ibn Faḍlān in 921, and that of the Spanish Jew *Ibn Ya'qūb to the court of Otto the Great. Travel-literature found a popular audience. The Arab has always been a wanderer, and his natural propensity, strengthened by the duty of Pilgrimage to Mecca, moves him to curiosity about foreign lands and peoples. The first of the early travellers' tales of India, Africa, and China which we possess is **The Chain of Histories*, compiled at the port of Sīrāf in 851 (apparently verbatim from various sources) with a supplement dating from about 910. Its ancient popularity in the East is reflected in the later West, where it was one of the earliest non-scientific books to be translated into a European language. The marvellous element is more prominent in its successor, **The Wonders of India*, written about 950 by a Persian ship-captain from Rām-hurmuz. Somewhat akin to this is a short compendium of geography and legendary history with special reference to Egypt, drawn largely from Mas'ūdī, known as **The Summary of Marvels*.

The immense development of prose-writing described in the preceding pages explains almost of itself the decline of poetry to a secondary place from now onwards. One of the first results of the new prose medium, with its superior flexibility and adaptation to social changes, was to displace poetry from its former social function and to restrict it more and more to a purely aesthetic role. Combined with this was the wide expansion of intellectual interests, with which the poets were unable to keep pace. They were prisoners of their own conventions, broadened out and diversified as these conventions had been during the first two centuries of Islam. To a certain extent they were also the prisoners of their society. In his private and occasional verse the poet was no doubt free to express himself as he pleased, but the doctrine which finally prevailed was that his major social function was to 'immortalize' his patron by his panegyrical *qaṣīdas*—a remarkable reversion to the tribal function of the pre-Islamic poet.

The most interesting poets of this century are, in consequence, those who made an effort to break through these conventions in different ways. Abū Tammām (d. 846), a self-taught Syrian, tried to revive the weighty sonority of bedouin poetry and to marry it to the *badīʿ* ornamentation of the poets of Iraq; at the same time he attempted to make his verse the vehicle of a more complex structure of thought. His poetry is in consequence often strained and overloaded, or alternatively relaxed to an excessive degree, although it has found warm admirers in both medieval and modern times. His fellow townsman and disciple, al-Buḥturī (d. 897), with a more natural gift, remained closer to the Iraqi tradition in his smoother and more polished verse. In Iraq, on the other hand, Ibn al-Rūmī (d. 896) attempted to create a new introspective and analytical poetry, in which each poem develops a single theme in an organic unity, and which has sometimes, but doubtfully, been genetically linked with his 'Greek' origin. The originality of this poetry (though marred by an excessive sense of grievance) was appreciated, but not imitated; and the more typical and influential representative of Iraqi modernism was the unlucky ʿAbbāsid prince Ibn al-Muʿtazz, whose caliphate of a day ended with his assassination in 908. With a freedom denied to those poets who had to earn their bread, he adapted traditional themes and metres to new uses, such as poetical 'Epistles' and descriptive verse. His innovations in technique and ingenuity include a *miniature epic in 450 iambic couplets celebrating the reign of his cousin, the Caliph al-Muʿtaḍid, and he was the first (and apparently the only) Arabic poet to compose a work on poetics, in which he classified the figures of speech employed in the 'new' poetry. Nevertheless, the total effect of his experiments was rather to revise than to reform the conventions within which the Arabic poet might apply his art.

§ 3. FROM A.D. 945 TO 1055

In the tenth century the dominating position of Baghdād and Iraq in Arabic letters was challenged by the successive emergence of new centres. As ʿAbbāsid control weakened, powerful new states were carved out of its former territories, and new dynasties were eager to enhance their reputation by bestowing their patronage on writers and poets. The event which more than any other symbolized this transformation of the political and cultural life of the Islamic Empire was the occupation of Baghdād in 945 by the Persian house of Buwaih and the reduction of the city of the caliphs to a provincial capital. The Buwaihids were Shiʿites, although they retained the ʿAbbāsid caliphate under their control, and in their territories, centring round the princely houses of Rayy, Fārs, and ʿIrāq, the tendencies repressed by the orthodox enjoyed almost untrammelled freedom. Shīʿism, indeed, was triumphant during the whole of this century from north Africa to the borders of eastern Persia, and under its protection the leaven of Hellenism produced some of its most brilliant results.

Parallel with the decentralization of Arabic literature, and intimately related to it, was the foundation of libraries and academies in all the great cities of the Muslim world. Princes and viziers vied with one another in procuring first editions and copies of valuable works, and in several centres provision was made for the upkeep of students and professors in particular disciplines. The details of these institutions make astounding reading. A minor college founded at Baghdād in 990 contained 10,400 books; the great library of the Fāṭimid caliph al-ʿAzīz at Cairo contained at the lowest estimate 120,000 volumes, while that of al-Ḥakam at Cordova was even larger. It has been suggested (although doubtfully) that it may be the catalogue of some such library that has come down to us by the name of *al-Fihrist* ('The Index'), composed by an-Nadīm at Baghdād in 988. This remarkable work opens with a section on various languages and scripts and the sacred books recognized by Muslims, followed by seven 'discourses' on the different branches of Arabic literature, philology, history, poetry, theology, law, philosophy, fables and magic, and adds two final discourses on sects and foreign religions, and alchemy. In each section the author enumerates all known books on these subjects with brief biographical notices of their authors and much other valuable material for the cultural history of the Near East. The *Fihrist* reveals to us how enormous was the output of Arabic literature in the first three centuries of Islam, and how very little has come down to us. Of many authors we possess only small fragments, and the great majority would otherwise have been entirely unknown to us even by name.

This immense development of literary production, seconded by the tireless activity of the philological schools, was bound to produce in due course a considerable volume of technical literary criticism, directed in the first instance towards poetry. The early philologists had, of course, freely expressed their view on the relative merits of given poets or verses, but mostly in the form of subjective judgements. The first steps towards a more systematic criticism had been taken by al-Jāḥiẓ (p. 75) and Ibn al-Muʿtazz (p. 86), and the rhetorician Qudāma b. Jaʿfar (d. 922) had introduced the classification of poetic 'beauties' and 'faults'. By the end of the tenth century Abū Hilāl al-ʿAskarī (d. 1005) offers a complete critical analysis of poetry and prose in terms of structure, rhetorical devices, and figures of speech. The significant feature of most of this discussion was the insistence on form rather than matter as the decisive criterion of quality; the declared assumption is that little if anything new can be originated in poetry, and that the only difference between one poet and another lies in his manner of expression. The balance was to some extent redressed by *ʿAbd al-Qāhir al-Jūrjānī (d. 1078), who supplemented the excessively formal analysis of his predecessors by a system of logical and psychological analysis which demanded at least equal consideration for the 'ideas' expressed. Additional point was given to the argument on literary aesthetics by its bearing on the doctrine of the incomparability of the Koran; inevitably, in spite of some protests in theological circles and by Jūrjānī, the prevailing concentration of criticism upon form tended to emphasize unduly its supreme verbal qualities in terms of the current stylistic theories.

A further consequence was that artistic and literary prose began to be affected by the same theories and to display the same pursuit of verbal elaboration. The virtuosity of the *adīb* was displayed in 'paragraphs' (*fuṣūl*) describing scenes, persons, emotions, events, and objects, or in 'epistles' (*rasā'il*) addressed to friends or colleagues on a variety of occasions. Ibn al-Muʿtazz seems to have been, if not the inventor, at least the popularizer of this art, which in the tenth century swept over the whole field of Arabic letters in the eastern provinces. The secretarial class fell victim to it almost at once; in the intense competition for office every refinement of literary style was eagerly exploited. The technique of secretarial correspondence was elaborated into the art of 'composition' (*inshā'*), based upon admired models of elegant, florid, insinuating, or pungent writing. It was not long before rhyme also was pressed into service. It seems that in early times a certain veneration had attached to rhymed prose (*sajʿ*), as the medium employed in the Koran, which militated against its general adoption for profane purposes, although for a century or two the official predication (*khuṭba*) on Fridays in the cathedral mosques had been moving in this direction. Saif ad-Dawla's court preacher Ibn Nubāta (d. 984), for instance, wrote his entire sermons in *sajʿ*; these, collected by his son, have always been highly esteemed for their style and contents. But by the middle of the tenth century the vizier Abu'l-Faḍl Ibn al-ʿAmīd (d. 969) was composing his official correspondence in *sajʿ*; with his disciple and successor, Ibn ʿAbbād, known as 'the Ṣāḥib' (d. 995), it was a mania, and henceforward it became inseparable from official composition. The best stylists still held aloof from its use except as occasional ornament and in writing prefaces; the geographer Maqdisī, writing in 985, declares that in his time 'men of letters prefer prose to rhythm but the vulgar love rhymes and *saj*''.

Nevertheless, the way once opened by secretarial *insha'*, so tempting an ornament of Arabic speech could not be permanently excluded from general literature, especially in a society of philologists, and it was rapidly introduced into most branches of belles-lettres to impart brilliance, wit, and polish. This was a momentous step in the development of Arabic prose. The additional premium which it placed on wit and agility produced, as we shall note in due course, not a few masterpieces of artistic invention by those who possessed a natural talent for it, but exacted in return a heavy price. The enforced cult of rhyme not only contorted the style of men of natural but more ponderous genius, like Abu'l-'Alā al-Ma'arrī (p. 92), but by rewarding artificiality it contributed to turning Arabic writers still farther away from the solid ground of real life and living issues and to sap the vitality of Arabic literature.

We turn now to survey the special developments of Arabic letters in the separate regions.

(*a*) *The circle of Saif ad-Dawla.* For a few brilliant years a new outburst of poetic genius brought enduring fame to the little Arab dynasty of the Ḥamdānids in northern Syria. The reputation and generosity of the warrior Saif ad-Dawla (*reg.* 944–67) attracted to Aleppo a pleiad of poets, all gifted in various ways, to contend for his favours. Among them was Saif ad-Dawla's own nephew *Abū Firās (d. 967), whose natural and relatively unadorned genius rises to genuine heights of emotion in the poems written during his captivity in Constantinople.

The outstanding figure among them, however, and the one to whom the 'circle' owes its special place in Arabic literature, was Abu'ṭ-Ṭayyib al-Mutanabbī (d. 965), claimed by some native critics to be the greatest of Arab poets, or at least the last great Arab poet. Mutanabbī, who owes his sobriquet ('The Would-be Prophet') to an escapade in early life, was of Kufan origin but Syrian in his poetical apprenticeship, and succeeded in blending the Arabian tradition of Abū Tammām with the smoothness and technical ingenuity of the 'Irāqī school. The boastful and overbearing nature openly displayed in his poems raised up against him a host of enemies and critics both in his lifetime and in later ages, but it is generally admitted that for skill in construction, felicity in language, and mastery of the lapidary phrase Mutanabbī has no equal among the later *qaṣīd*-poets.

Unlike most earlier *qaṣīdas*, Mutanabbī's odes are usually constructed as organic wholes, with theme passing into theme in a natural and ordered succession. This quality of his art, curiously enough, was seldom appreciated by Arab critics, who (following the old tradition) often pick out single verses for praise or blame without regard to their relation to the contextual pattern. At the same time, no other poet has contributed so much to the common stock of poetical quotations in Arabic letters.

The measure of the resolute is seen in their resolves
 As generous deeds display the worth of noble souls.

Honour the man of noble soul, he becomes your slave,
 But the mean-souled man when honoured grows insolent.

Naught will suffice for the understanding of men
 When the light of day itself stands in need of proof.

Whoso desires the ocean makes light of streams.

Men bury and are buried, and our feet
Trample the skulls of those who went before.

In the background of this brilliant society, and scarcely heeded by them, lived one of the greatest of Muslim thinkers, al-Fārābī (d. 950), of central-Asian Turkish descent. His works on medicine and music became standard treatises, but it is for his services to Arabic philosophy that his name still lives. His chief endeavour was to reconcile the systems of Aristotle and Plato (as interpreted chiefly by the Neoplatonists), but with all this he remained a firm believer in the truth of Islam and strove to bring the whole of Greek philosophy into conformity with its doctrines. His most interesting work for us is **The Opinions of the Citizens of the Virtuous City*, which may be described as a short Muslim version of the *Republic*, conceived as both Church and State in one.

The north Syrian school came to an end soon after the death of Saif ad-Dawla, but one belated figure connected with it remains to be mentioned. Abu'l-ʿAlā al-Maʿarrī (973–1057) is a solitary and unexpected apparition in Arabic literature. Though blind from his youth, he studied in Aleppo and for a short time tried his fortune in Baghdād, but retired in the end to his native town of Maʿarra. In his earlier poems, collected under the title of *Saqṭ az-Zand*, he was a follower of Mutanabbī, but in his later poems, for all the complicated artifice in rhyme and word-harmony implied in their technical name of **Luzūmīyāt*, he broke with convention and stands out as a great humanist and an incisive, though pessimistic, thinker.

Taking reason for his guide [says R. A. Nicholson] he judges men and things with a freedom which must have seemed scandalous to the rulers and privileged classes of the day. Amid his meditations on the human tragedy a fierce hatred of injustice, hypocrisy, and superstition blazes out. Vice and folly are laid bare in order that virtue and wisdom may be sought. In his poetry we see the age depicted without fear or favour, and—what is more appealing—the artist himself, struggling with doubts, yet confident in the power of mind to solve difficulties and give light, if any can be looked for. But much of the *Luzūm* is monotonous; a great deal is trivial and pedantic and to our taste intolerably clever; it moves us to admiration and contempt, it thrills, fatigues, fascinates, and repels; and when all has been said, it remains unique and immortal because it expresses the personality of an extraordinary man.

> They all err—Moslem, Christian, Jew, and Magian;
> Two make Humanity's universal sect:
> One man intelligent without religion,
> And one religious without intellect.[1]

His Muslim contemporaries, although they flocked to his lectures, did not know quite what to make of him, and their successors, finding in the *Luzūmīyāt* much that displeased them, as Muslims, in Abu'l-ʿAlā's philosophic scepticism and detached attitude to all formal religion, and as aesthetes, in his disregard of the traditional canons of Arabic poetry, have generally ranked the *Saqṭ az-Zand* higher. Some modern critics have gone to the opposite extreme and credited him with advanced philosophical views which he himself would probably have repudiated with horror. Of his prose writings the most celebrated is 'The Epistle of Pardon' (*Risālat al-Ghufrān*). About 1025 a Spanish-Arab writer, Ibn Shuhaid, had composed a series of imaginary interviews with the *jinnīs* who inspired (according to the ancient Arab conception) the great poets of the past. Whether he knew of this work or not,

[1] R. A. Nicholson, *Eastern Poetry and Prose*, p. 110.

Abu'l-'Alā some eight years later more daringly imagined in his *Epistle* a visit to heaven and hell to interview the poets themselves. This extravaganza, with its ironical overtones, is somewhat spoiled for us by the philological pedantry with which he burdened it, as is also a collection of **Letters* made by the author himself and composed in a heavy style of rhymed prose, abounding in allusions and literary 'graces'. Even more formidable is the display of philological erudition in a controversial work, recently recovered in part, entitled 'Paragraphs and Periods' (*al-Fuṣūl wa 'l-Ghāyāt*), in elaborately interwoven rhymed prose, so complicated and obscure that none but his own pupils were said to understand it. Ostensibly composed 'to celebrate the glory of God and to admonish', each paragraph spins around a core of Koranic maxims and pious exhortations a fantastic web of pessimistic and often ironical observations on nature and human life. Scandalized orthodox scholars denounced it as a parody of the Koran; it is scarcely that, but what Abu'l-'Alā really meant by it remains an unsolved problem.

(*b*) *Iraq under the Buwaihids.* While the native Arab elements in Muslim literature still governed the circle of Saif ad-Dawla, in Baghdād they were by now completely fused into the cosmopolitan culture of medieval Islam and beginning to be affected by the revival of Persian literature and taste in the East. In lieu of the nonentities who held the Caliphate, and the rough Buwaihid rulers, the patronage of letters fell to a series of remarkable and immensely wealthy Persian viziers. Most famous of them all is 'the Ṣāḥib', Ibn 'Abbād (938–95), whose 'salon' was graced by most of the poets, writers, and scientists of the age.

The two outstanding literary figures of the Buwaihid

period are the historian Miskawaih (d. 1030) and the essayist Abū Ḥayyān at-Tawḥīdī (d. 1023). The former, in addition to an influential work on ethics, largely based on but developing the synthesis of Islamic and Hellenistic thought by al-Kindī (p. 65), produced in **The Experiences of the Nations* the first important general history since Ṭabarī. Its significance in Arabic literature is that Miskawaih was not, like Ṭabarī and most of his predecessors, a scholar versed in the theological and philological sciences but an official and courtier, and the latter part of his work illustrates the new direction of historical composition towards contemporary annalistic, based on official documents and personal contacts. Although this opened the door, as we shall shortly see, to many abuses, Miskawaih himself was a serious scholar with an exacting standard of accuracy and relative independence of judgement, allowing for some natural hero-worship of his first patron, the vizier Ibn al-ʿAmīd.

A very different note is struck by his friend Tawḥīdī (we possess an interesting correspondence on philosophical topics between them), who, although all but forgotten until a few years ago, ranks with Jāḥiẓ as a master of Arabic prose, 'the imām of the eloquent [says Yāqūt], unique and unrivalled in sagacity, intelligence, mastery of style and vigour'. In his *Book of the Two Viziers* he portrayed the weaknesses of Ibn al-ʿAmīd and the Ṣāḥib with such bitterness that the book was reputed to bring misfortune upon all who possessed a copy. The following passage on the Ṣāḥib, from a partial draft preserved in one of his other books, may serve as a sample:

He used to write verses at festivals and other occasions and send them to Abū ʿĪsā, son of the astrologer, saying, 'I make you a present of this qaṣīda; recite it in my praise when the poets are assembled'. So Abū 'Īsā, who was a hard-bitten Baghdādī and an old hand at tricks and ruses, would come and recite, and the Ṣāḥib, on hearing himself lauded to the skies in verses of his own concoction, would say, 'Recite that again, Abū 'Isā. Go ahead, Abū 'Īsā. You are a fine poet now, by God; your talents and imagination have matured and your rhymes are impeccable, not like the sort of thing you recited at the last festival. Our salon—that is what turns out men, polishes their intelligence and natural gifts, and transforms the draught horse into a courser.' And with that he would never dismiss him without giving him a handsome reward, while the poets and others present gnashed their teeth, well aware that Abū 'Īsā was incapable of composing half a line without bungling.

Several of Tawḥīdī's books and treatises have been recovered and published in recent years, the most remarkable being *The Book of Enlivenment and Good Company*, a touched-up record of 'conversations' on all sorts of literary, philosophical, and scientific subjects among a group of friends at the evening 'salon' of another vizier. This three-volume work not only displays Tawḥīdī as indeed a master of Arabic prose but also captures and records with wit and irony the tone of the sophisticated literary society of Baghdād at its culminating moment.

The Buwaihid period produced also, in addition to continuations of the histories of Ṭabarī and Miskawaih, three notable works in the related field of biography. A student of the *Ḥadith*, known as 'The Preacher of Baghdād' (d. 1071), compiled in fourteen volumes the biographies of over 7,000 scholars, poets, writers, and political figures connected with Baghdād, one of the first of the comprehensive biographical dictionaries which are among the most remarkable productions of the later centuries of Islamic culture. Hilāl aṣ-Ṣābi' (d. 1056) belongs to the school of Miskawaih; his *Book of Viziers*, only partly preserved, is a candid account of the bureaucracy of Baghdād in the tenth century, based on and often quoting the actual documents. The third work, the *Book of Songs* of Abu'l-Faraj al-Iṣfahānī (d. 967), has already been mentioned (p. 25). The author's critical judgement and reliability in details may perhaps be questioned, but the immense panorama of Arabian and early Islamic life and manners presented in his twenty volumes is probably unequalled in any literature down to modern times.

In the general field of belles-lettres, however, the fashion of the time was all for jingling rhymes and entertainment. It was now that the first drafts of the *Arabian Nights* were made with tales translated from Indian and Persian, and it was with the same object that men of letters ransacked literature for anecdotes to be substituted for the philological and scholastic contents of the essay. Such anecdotal collections, of course, have always been immensely popular, from the earliest productions of the qaḍī aṭ-Ṭanūkhī (940–94), called *Deliverance after Distress* and **The Collection of Histories*, through an innumerable progeny (of which **The Literary Delectus* [*al-Mustaṭraf*] of al-Abshīhī [1388–1446] may be cited here as one of the best both in contents and style) down to our own day. The fashion passed even into history, when Ibrāhīm aṣ-Ṣābi' (d. 994), ordered by his Buwaihid master to write a history of the dynasty, produced in rhymed prose a bombastic (and needless to say untruthful) eulogy, now apparently lost, and set thereby an example for many later generations of Persian dynastic chroniclers. It may be more than a coincidence that this production was contemporary with the creation of the Persian epic and revival of the royal annals in the East (p. 103).

Another sign of the times was the vogue of popular poetry (although in the literary language), of which, for the first time in the history of Arabic literature, several specimens have been preserved in a more or less fragmentary state.

The remaining literature of the Buwaihid period is mainly on religious and related topics. The term would hardly cover the famous treatise on the **Principles of Government* by the qāḍī al-Māwardī (d. 1058), were it not that it is a programme for the ideal government of the theocratic state with but slight concessions to what the theologians regarded as the corrupt and illegal practice of the day. The Shiʿites, of course, made the most of their opportunity of open activity, and the bibliography of Shiʿite books composed by the jurist Muḥammad aṭ-Ṭūsī (d. 1067) is of interest as showing the volume of Shiʿite literature then existing that has since perished, the greater part no doubt suppressed by the orthodox Sunnīs. Somewhat before this, however, the Zaidī sect of the Shīʿa had founded an independent state in the Yemen, which has maintained its existence to this day. In this secluded corner they produced a considerable literature whose monuments are only now being investigated and found to possess, in spite of their predominant theological content, no little interest and value. Of the general literary work of the Shiʿites special interest attaches to the pseudographs attributed to the Prophet's son-in-law ʿAlī, but written by two brothers, the Sharīfs (i.e. descendants of ʿAlī) al-Murtaḍā (966–1044) and ar-Raḍī (970–1015), the latter of whom was one of the most noted poets of the day. These forgeries consist of a poetic *dīwān* and a work containing, under the title of *The Highway of Eloquence*, the supposed sermons and letters of ʿAlī. The latter work in particular, written in pleasing and not too ornate *saj'*, has enjoyed a great reputation not only among the Shi'ites (who revere it as an authentic monument of their Imām) but also among Sunnī Muslims. Another famous didactic ode attributed to 'Alī, known as the **Zainab Ode*, is an earlier forgery by one of the minor poets of the early 'Abbāsid period.

While these writers belong to the major Shi'ite sect of the 'Twelvers' or 'Imamites', the Shi'ite name had also been used to cover another movement, apparently philosophical in its origins, out of which arose, in the political sphere, the Fāṭimid dynasty (p. 107) and its still extremer offshoot, the secret society in Persia and Syria known as the 'Assassins'. The literature of this Isma'īlī movement, which includes at least two interesting memoirs as well as historical and theological works, has gradually emerged from its jealously guarded concealment in the last 20 years. But one work of Ismā'īlī inspiration, the **Epistles of the Pure Brethren*, enjoyed a more general reputation. These fifty-one treatises, compiled by a group of writers in Baṣra some time before the year 1,000, form an encyclopaedia of science and philosophy, summarizing the ideas of cultured Muslim society in the tenth century. By this time orthodox scholarship was moving towards a compromise with philosophy, much on the lines of the similar compromise in medieval Europe, on condition that its doctrines were not pushed to their extreme conclusions. The epistles of the 'Pure Brethren' (*Ikhwān aṣ-Ṣafā*), by their observance of these limits, were assured of general acceptance and have found an audience in all Muslim countries, both in the original text and in extracts and translations. The treatises begin with mathematics (nos. 1–6), introduction to philosophy and logic (nos. 7–13), and pass on to the general sciences (nos. 14–21) and anthropology (nos. 22–30). So far the teachings are based almost entirely on Aristotle. The next section, on the 'World-soul' (nos. 31–40), is clearly Neoplatonic, and the final treatises deal with the 'theological sciences' in, as might be expected, a strongly Muʿtazilite vein.

(*c*) *Eastern Persia.* Although the Persian dynasties in the East favoured the revival of Persian as a literary language, Arabic was still largely used in court circles and official correspondence, and Arabic poets and writers found a ready patronage extended to them. The most brilliant of the eastern courts was that of the Sāmānids at Bukhārā, but the wealthy trading centre of Khwārizm (now Khiva) was particularly celebrated for its devotion to learning. The Oxus provinces were always famed for their zeal in religious studies, and of the compilers of the canonical books of Tradition the majority, including both Bukhārī and Muslim, belonged to Khurāsān.

With Nīshāpūr, the capital of Khurāsān proper, are connected the two most brilliant belle-lettrists of this period, al-Hamadhānī (969–1008) and ath-Thaʿālibī (961–1038). The former, more generally known as Badīʿ az-Zamān ('The Wonder of the Age'), passed his life travelling from one court to another, from the day when he left Hamadhān at the age of twelve, having already learned all that his teachers had to teach him, till his death at Herāt. An extract from Thaʿālibī's account of him is interesting not only in itself, but as a picture of the recreations of lettered society in his day, and it will help us also to understand the success of his **Maqāmāt*.

He was a master of marvels and ingenuities. He would recite a poem of more than fifty lines which he had never heard but once, remember it all and repeat it all from beginning to end without altering a letter. He would skim over four or five pages of a book he did not know and had never seen, then repeat it from memory perfectly co-ordinated. He would be asked to compose a poem on some original or out-of-the-way point, and would acquit himself of the task on the spot. He used often to write a book on the subject set him, beginning at the end and finishing at the beginning, and yet produce a work as beautiful and witty as any. He would adorn a choice *qaṣīda* with a noble treatise both of his own composition, read out of poetry prose, and fashion out of prose poetry. He would be given many rhymes, and would fit elegant verses to them, or be set to compose in prose or verse on all sorts of abstruse and difficult subjects, and recite extemporaneously, quicker than a flash. He could translate Persian verses full of conceits into Arabic verses with both speed and brilliance, and do many other marvellous things past numbering.

By this time the employment of rhymed prose in literary 'epistles', introduced into the eastern provinces by Abū Bakr al-Khwārizmī (d. 1002), was spreading like wildfire, and in Hamadhānī, with such resources at his disposal, the new art found an unsurpassed exponent. But his position in Arabic literature is assured less by his ingenious *Epistles* than as the creator of its most perfect form of literary presentation, the *Maqāma* or 'Assembly'. The hand of its originator determined once and for all its setting.

He imagined [says Chenery] a witty, unscrupulous improviser wandering from place to place and living on the presents which the display of his gifts produced from the generous and tasteful, and a kind of Rāwī or narrator, who should be continually meeting with the other, should relate his adventures and repeat his excellent compositions. . . .The Assembly is a kind of dramatic anecdote in the telling of which the author's object is to display his poetry, his eloquence, or his learning, and with this view the subject is continually subordinated to the treatment, the substance to the form.

Some philologists had already adopted the anecdote as a means to enliven the presentation of their more recondite linguistic researches. What Hamadhānī did was to expand this pedantic invention into the old-time tale in alternate prose and verse (the type of which is represented in European literature by *Aucassin and Nicolette*), to invest it with the literary graces of *saj'* and the glamour of impromptu composition, and, by a stroke of genius, to adopt as the mouthpiece of his art that familiar figure in popular story, the witty vagabond. His hero, Abu'l-Fatḥ of Alexandria, is represented as possessing all the arts of rhetoric and nimbleness of wit with which, as we have seen, Hamadhānī himself was endowed. Learned and unlearned alike were united in admiration of his work, and, as its fame spread throughout the Arab world, it found many imitators, but the *maqāma* never regained the spontaneity and mobility which, for all its elaboration of technique, it possessed in the hands of its talented creator. It has been suggested by a modern critic that the *maqāma* represents in Semitic literature the culminating stage in the presentment of the literary theme.

There is at bottom the same series of stages of increasing 'mobilization' of the literary theme among Aryans and Semites: epic (= *qaṣīda*), drama (= *qiṣṣa*, the alternative prose and verse tale), novel (= *maqāma*). At the first stage the memory alone of the auditor is brought into play; at the second the actor or reciter challenges the intelligence of the hearer; at the third it is to the will itself of the reader that appeal is made. Only, with the Aryan the form is capricious and the substance is fixed; while with the Semite the form is rigid and the substance capricious and unreal.[1]

[1] L. Massignon, *Lexique de la Mystique musulmane*, p. 298.

For all his admiration of the genius of Hamadhānī, Tha'ālibī followed the more beaten tracks of philology and *adab*. His importance for us rests mainly on two books. One is a *general history, of which only the portion dealing with the early kings of Persia has come down to us, but which is of interest in that it presents the last independent prose version of the material which was simultaneously being worked up by the great Persian poet Firdawsī to its final expression in the famous Persian epic, the *Shāhnāma*. The other is a biographical anthology of poets and writers of the preceding century or so, presenting their most successful verses, literary 'paragraphs', and metaphorical descriptions and imagery, under the title of *The Solitaire of the Age*. Thanks to the fine critical taste of its author, the collection gained an immediate success, and was supplemented by a series of continuators during the next two centuries.

When in 999 the Samanids were ousted by the Central Asian Turks, their mantle fell on the new Turkish dynasty established at Ghazna in Afghanistan. The most famous of the Ghaznevid princes, Maḥmūd Yamīn ad-Dawla (*reg.* 998–1030), although an illiterate barbarian at heart, ostentatiously sought renown in the political field by carrying fire and sword into India under a thin disguise of religious zeal, and in literature by bringing the chief writers of the day to add glitter and pomp to his court. In what was probably deliberate emulation of Ibrāhīm aṣ-Ṣābi' and his history of the Buwaihids (p. 97), one of his court officials, al-'Utbī (d. 1036), celebrated his reign in an adulatory rhymed-prose monograph, *The Book of Yamīn ad-Dawla*, which remained for centuries a much admired model, especially in the East. This had deplorable consequences. Even when the writers of such 'official histories' may be acquitted of deliberate falsehood, or of the more common vices of servility and *suppressio veri*, their aim is to dazzle rather than to inform; rhetoric is piled upon rhetoric and trope upon trope until simple fact is lost in a mist of obscurity and bombast. Unfortunately, the literary reputation of several of these works has often caused them to be regarded as representative of Islamic history in general, a view which is patently unjust to the sobriety of both sense and style in all but a minority of Arabic historians.

Maḥmūd did not rely on his reputation for generosity to attract scholars and men of letters. His method was cheaper and more effective: he kidnapped them or exacted them as tribute from the states he conquered. It was thus that, on the conquest of Khwārizm, he became the patron of al-Bīrūnī (d. 1048), who, more than any other writer, represents for us the genius of Islamic science. In his eyes exact knowledge was an end in itself.

When he compiled his *Canon* (says an authority quoted by Yāqūt) the Sultan (Masʿūd) rewarded him with an elephant load of silver, but he broke with custom and returned it to the treasury, pleading his ability to do without it. His hand was scarcely ever separated from a pen, or his eye from observation, or his mind from thought except on the two festival days of the year, Nairūz and Mihrjān. On all other days his constant preoccupation was to remove the veil of dubiety from the face of knowledge and roll up the sleeves of constraint from its forearms. A certain learned man said: I visited Abu'r-Raiḥān (Bīrūnī) as he was on the point of giving up his soul and his breath was at the death-rattle and he, in that condition, said to me, 'How was it that you once explained to me a certain problem of inheritance?' I said to him sympathetically, 'In this condition?' and he replied, 'Is it not better that I should bid farewell to the world knowing this question than that I should leave it without this knowledge?' So I repeated it to him and he memorized it and taught me what he had promised; then I went out and even as I was in the street I heard the cry announcing his death.

Of his historical and philosophical works, unfortunately, nothing has been preserved, but his fame is securely founded on three masterpieces of compilation. **The Surviving Monuments of Past Generations* is a study in comparative chronology embracing not only a description of the eras and festivals of various nations and religions, but a good deal of historical information and curious observations on many subjects. For the second work he took advantage of Maḥmūd's conquests in India to learn Sanskrit and study Indian literature, and produced as the fruit of thirteen years of labour a work on India which in subject and scientific method stands alone in Arabic literature. In his Chronology he had shown himself an exact scholar, in the **India* he went further and proved himself able to rise above national and religious prejudice (except perhaps a native grudge against the Arabs), and to hold an even balance between uncritical admiration and unthinking aversion. He translated many Indian books (including the Yoga Sutra and Patanjali, a copy of which has survived) into Arabic, and, more curiously, several Arabic translations from the Greek into Sanskrit. The third compilation, considered by some as his greatest work, summarizes under the title of *The Canon dedicated to Masʿūd* (Maḥmūd's son and successor), the entire astronomical science of the Arabs in twelve volumes, and was supplemented by a shorter *compendium on astrology.

A very different type of scholar, although no less gifted and dedicated, was Ibn Sīnā (980–1037) of Bukhārā. After a breathless flight from Khwārizm to escape the clutches of Maḥmūd, and an adventurous political career, he settled finally in Iṣfahān. 'Avicenna' long represented to western eyes the climax of Islamic science, but in our Middle Ages and now again in this century he is celebrated first and foremost as a philosopher (as were indeed most Muslim doctors). He is credited in the latest list of his writings with no fewer than 46 philosophical works, as against 44 on medicine and 81 on astronomy and the natural sciences. In the first category falls his *Book of Healing* (i.e. of the Soul), an encyclopaedia of logic, physics, mathematics, and metaphysics (or theology), and one of the most stimulating and most debated works of medieval philosophy among both Christian schoolmen and later Muslim metaphysicians, especially in Persia. In strange contrast to the basically Aristotelian intellectualism of his philosophy, he wrote also some seventy works on religious subjects; and not only so, but a number of mystical works written in his later years, mostly in the form of *symbolic tales and romances, as well as a charming short poem on the *Descent of the Soul into the Body, played a major part in stimulating the future 'oriental philosophy' and 'illuminationist' Ṣūfism of the East. His European reputation, however, and much of his renown in the Muslim world, rested on his medical works, and more especially the voluminous medical encyclopaedia called *The Canon*, which governed European medicine for several centuries after its translation by Gerard of Cremona in the thirteenth century. Even among Muslims it ousted the works of Avicenna's predecessors, and combined with his reputation in philosophy to place its author on a pedestal above even the more original genius of Rāzī (p. 66).

(*d*) *Egypt and north-west Africa.* During the first three centuries of Islam, Arabic literary culture in Egypt was mainly reflected from Madīna and Baghdād. In the ninth century, however, there arose an independent group of historians, both Muslim and Christian, several of whose works have been preserved. In north-west Africa the development of a literary culture was even slower; as late as the tenth century it was only at Qairawān in Tunisia that the existence of an active centre of Mālikī legal studies stimulated a growing literary activity. The advent of the Shiʿite Fāṭimid dynasty (p. 99), which established itself in Tunisia in 909 and in Egypt sixty years later, did little to disturb intellectual intercourse with the East, but Egypt seems to have remained relatively unaffected by the influences that were remoulding Arabic literature in ʿIrāq and Persia. Apart from the recently recovered *dīwān* of one major poet, the Andalusian Ibn Hāni' (d. 973), the panegyrist of the Fāṭimid caliph al-Mu'izz, little that survives of the works produced there during this period is of general interest. The Fāṭimids were, nevertheless, munificent patrons of learning. One of their first acts in Egypt was to erect and endow the college mosque of al-Azhar, which, after its reversion to orthodoxy and the destruction of its chief rivals in Asia, became, and remains to this day, the chief university in Islam. The apparent poverty of Egyptian literature under their rule may plausibly be put down to the suppression or disregard by later orthodox circles of everything tinged with the Fāṭimid heresy. The geographer Maqdisī in fact, writing in 985, says outright:

> Baghdād was in former times an illustrious city, but it is now crumbling to decay and its glory has departed. I found neither pleasure nor aught worthy of admiration there. Cairo today is what Baghdād was in its prime, and I know of no more illustrious city in Islam.

(*e*) *Spain* (750–1091). The development of an Arabic literature in Spain was delayed by many factors. Lying on the extreme perimeter of the Islamic world, Spain lacked also an organized central government such as the ʿAbbāsids had created in the East. The struggles between the Arabs and the Berbers and the factions that rent the Arabs themselves produced an atmosphere that but little favoured literary pursuits. More important still, the outside influences that had so powerfully contributed to the development of an Arabic literature in Iraq and Persia had no parallel in the barbarian Gothic kingdom which the Muslims had overthrown. In the East the Arab conquerors became the disciples of the conquered; in Spain it was the Gothic Christians who adopted the civilization of the Arabs. The Umayyad princes strove, by their enlightened and generous patronage, to attract eastern scholars to their court and succeeded in making their new capital, Cordova, the centre from which the Muslim civilization radiated even beyond the frontiers of Spain. The culminating moment of their power, the reign of the illustrious ʿAbd ar-Raḥmān III (912–61), marks also the period when the genius of the Spanish Muslims, so long in germinating, found itself, to produce during the following centuries a series of men of letters whose works are among the most brilliant memorials of the Muslim civilization.

As in north-west Africa, Andalusian literature begins with studies in Mālikī law and theology, and the first Spanish author in the field of belles-lettres is Ibn ʿAbd Rabbihi (860–940), a freedman of the Umayyad family. His only work, apart from some poetry, was *al-ʿIqd al-Farīd* ('The Unique Necklace'), a famous literary thesaurus on the lines of and to a considerable extent derived from

Ibn Qutaiba's *Fountains of Story* (p. 77), filled out, as the author states in his preface, by 'conceits from my own poetry, that the reader may learn that our Western land, for all its distance and isolation, has a share in both poetry and prose'. The *'Iqd*, partly in consequence of its greater elaboration and simpler arrangement, completely supplanted Ibn Qutaiba's work, even in the East, and has remained to this day among the most popular works of recreation. While Ibn 'Abd Rabbihi was in the first place an aesthete, his successor was a philologist and ranks as the founder of the Spanish school of philology. Al-Qālī (d. 967) was born in Armenia and studied in Baghdād. In 942 he established himself in Cordova, where he spent the remaining years of his life and, among other works, delivered his *Dictations*, which are still widely read in the East. They consist of grammatical and lexicographical dissertations on various subjects, such as Koranic passages, old Arab tales, historical narratives and the like, with citations of traditions and verses of poetry.

Of the earliest Spanish–Arabic poets we know little, but enough to make it certain that, as might be expected, the traditional poetry was cultivated there also. The 'new style' too was carried over to Spain by the tenth century, as evidenced by Ibn 'Abd Rabbihi's naīve boast. Towards the beginning of the eleventh century, however, a new and native art began to appear. We have seen that in the East the literary poets took no account of popular tendencies; whatever failed to conform to the established literary usages was ruled out of court. Although this doctrine was never quite superseded even in Spain, new strophic forms were forcing a way into Andalusian poetry. The earliest to win a footing was the *muwashshaḥ* ('the girdled'), an arrangement in four-, five-, or six-line strophes, capable of wide variations in construction and rhyme, a typical scheme being *aa bbbaa cccaa*, &c., the final *aa* of the last strophe constituting a kind of *envoi*. The causes which led to the development of the strophe in Spain and not in the East are obscure; the influence of popular songs in Romance has long been suspected, and is reinforced by the recent discovery that in the earliest *muwashshaḥs* the *envoi* was actually in Romance. Some part may be due also to the special developments in the West of Arabic music (in Arabic *ṭarab*, the probable connexion of which with 'trobador' is too tempting not to note in passing).

The Arabic taste for elaboration on the one hand, and standardization on the other, is nowhere more strongly displayed than in the conventions which soon governed the art of the *muwashshaḥ*. The literary language was used throughout the poem, but it was regarded as a particular ornament if the *envoi* were sharp and pungent, and in colloquial speech. The lighter of the regular Arabic metres were generally employed, sometimes slightly modified to suit Andalusian rhythms, but the lines were broken up into sections of different length which rhymed internally throughout the strophe. It is not surprising that with these technical difficulties to overcome the later type of *muwashshaḥ* lacked spontaneity and, especially after its transference to the East, rapidly degenerated into a mechanical exercise, as stereotyped and artificial as the *qaṣīda*. The writer of *muwashshaḥs* was, it would seem, limited by yet another convention in his choice of subject. Rarely does a *muwashshaḥ* treat of anything but love, unless in religious poetry. Even in panegyric the form of addressing a lover is often retained. There are, of course, frequent reminiscences of and actual borrowings from the early poets, especially from 'Omar b. Abī Rabī'a (p. 44);

it was a common exercise to compose a new poem to the first line and *envoi* of an earlier poet, and the later poets freely plundered their predecessors' *muwashshaḥs*.

To translate a *muwashshaḥ* poem in a manner that reproduces the original is all but impossible, but the following version of a famous piece[1] may convey some idea of the technique.

My heaving sighs proclaim   Love's joys are bitterness.

My heart has lost her mentor,
She spurns my anguished cry
And craves for her tormentor;
If I hide love, I die.

When 'Oh heart!' I exclaim   My foes mock my distress.

O tearful one who chantest
Of mouldering ditch and line,
Or hopefully decantest,
I have no eyes for thine.

Let yearning glow aflame,   Tears pour in vain excess.

Mine eye, love's tribute venting,
Expended all its store,
Then its own pain lamenting
Began to weep once more.

My heart is past reclaim   Or sweet forgetfulness.

I blame it not for weeping
My heart's distress to share,
As, weary but unsleeping,
It probed the starry sphere.

[1] By the physician Abū Bakr Ibn Zuhr, son of the celebrated 'Abenzoar'. The metre of the original is *ab ccc ab ddd ab*, &c., ten syllables to each rhyming segment. The first *ab* was repeated after each recurrence except the last.

To count them was my aim But they are numberless.

A doe there was I trysted
(No lion is as tough).
I came, but she insisted
'Tomorrow', and sheered off.

Hey, folks, d'you know that game? And what's the gal's address?

The older forms, however, never lost their dominant position, and there were probably few poets who devoted themselves exclusively to the strophe. The stilted phrase and far-fetched conceit flourished as rankly as in the East; it would be hard to match this line from a Spanish panegyric:

How do his underclothes not waste away,
since he is a full moon [in beauty] and they are of cotton?

Even the hardened biographer Ibn Khallikān finds it necessary to explain that cotton is said to rot on exposure to moonlight.

The Golden Age of Andalusian poetry extends a few years beyond the limits we have set in the East. The decay of the Umayyad dynasty (*c.* 1020) and disintegration of Muslim Spain into a number of petty kingdoms seemed only to increase the literary and poetic activity of the age by establishing a dozen courts instead of one. Of the many poets of the eleventh century the two best known are *Ibn Zaidūn of Cordova (1003–71), who ranks generally as the greatest of the Spanish poets, both in his early love-songs and in the poetical epistles of his later life, and al-Muʿtamid (1040–95), the last native ruler of Seville. Both owe something of their fame to the circumstances of their lives, the former to his adventurous career and romantic attachment to the Umayyad princess Wallāda, the latter to the contrast between the magnificence of his court, when he ruled as *primus inter pares* among the kings of Spain, and his pitiful death as a captive in Morocco. But both (like many others of their fellow countrymen) were men for whom 'the most trivial and transient events of life instantly clothed themselves in a poetic form', and it is a matter for regret that relatively little of this most charming (to our taste) of all Arabic poetry has found adequate translation into English. Ibn Zaidūn is equally noted as a prose writer, partly for his letters, but more especially for his *Epistle* to his rival Ibn ʿAbdūs, a consummate piece of literary craftsmanship and biting satire. The following verses are from one of his later strophic poems:

Still round thy towers descend the fertile rain!
Still sing the doves in every leafy den!
Córdova, fairest home of gallant men,
Where youth my childhood's trinkets snapped in twain[1]
    And noble sires begat me noble, free!

Happy those days with purer pleasures blest,
Those winding vales we roamed with boyish zest,
White-throated, raven-haired, all mirth and jest;
Chide not the trailing robes, the silken vest,
    The reckless pride of youth—no wantons we.

Say to an age whose joys long since are fled,
Its traces by the lapse of nights now faint and mouldered
(Softly the breeze its evening fragrance shed!
Bright shone its stars o'er the night-traveller's head!):
    'Farewell from one whose love still burns for thee!'

In the eleventh century native schools of mathematics

[1] A reference to the practice of hanging amulets round the necks of young children.

and astronomy began to flourish in various parts of Muslim Spain. Somewhat earlier the medical science of the East had laid the foundations of the famous Spanish school of physicians (among them the celebrated family of Ibn Zuhr [Abenzoar], one of whom was the author of the *muwashshaḥ* rendered above), and the gift of an illustrated copy of the *Materia medica* of Dioscorides by a Greek emperor to ʿAbd ar-Raḥmān III stimulated the work of a series of celebrated botanists. But the chief figure in the prose literature of this century is Ibn Ḥazm of Cordova (994–1064), the grandson of a Spanish convert. In his early years he was a poet, whose genius was displayed less in his output of verse than in a delicate anatomy of chivalrous love, **Ṭawq al-Ḥamāma* ('The Dove's Neckring'), one of the few works of Arabic literature with an immediate and universal appeal. It is strange that it was this same Ibn Ḥazm who, belonging to the narrowest school of Islamic theology, devoted much of the rest of his literary activity to bitter attacks on his theological opponents; the sharpness of his tongue, which became proverbially linked with the sword of the tyrant al-Ḥajjāj, eventually forced him to give up political life and brought about his practical excommunication. Of his many religious and historical treatises few have survived, but among these is his valuable and original work on Comparative Religion (*The Book of Religious and Philosophical Sects*). Surprising though it may seem that it is in Arabic literature that we find the first works on this subject, the reasons for it are not far to seek. The tolerance of the Arab conquerors had left in their midst large communities holding varied religious opinions, Jews, Christians, Zoroastrians, and even semi-pagans. Their beliefs attracted the attention of Muslim scholars at an early date and led first to a large controversial literature (as a specimen of which may be cited the ***Book of Religion and Empire* written about 855 by ʿAli b. Rabban aṭ-Ṭabari, himself a convert from Christianity) and later on to a more scientific curiosity about them. There were also administrative problems connected with the special taxation and jurisdictions of the non-Muslims, which made it necessary for officials to have some knowledge of their creeds and practices. The rise of different canonical schools within the Islamic community itself led to the writing of works on comparative doctrine, generally with a controversial purpose, such as the *Distinction between the Sects* of Abū Manṣur* al-Baghdādī (d. 1037), which does not deal with any group beyond those who claimed to be included in Islam. It was reserved for Ibn Ḥazm, however, to write the first systematic and critical work on the religions of mankind, including their various sects and schools. His book opens with a theologico-philosophical classification of religions according to their beliefs on the origin of the world and the vocation of prophets; Christianity, for instance, comes under the category of creeds which assert that the world was created in time and had more than one creator, and which reject certain of the prophets (i.e. Muḥammad and the Arabian prophets). In each section he details the arguments advanced in support of these beliefs and follows them up with a refutation point by point. A large section of the book is devoted to a trenchant analysis, quoting chapter and verse, of the inconsistencies and, to the Muslim mind, absurdities contained in the Old and New Testaments. The various Muslim sects and philosophical schools are then discussed, and the work ends with an exposition of Ibn Ḥazm's own philosophical and theological views. It is clear that the purpose and style of the whole book is controversial, but it led to more judicial works on the same subject (p. 126).

It was natural that the Spanish historians should direct their attention almost exclusively to the history of the Arabs in Spain. The standard works written in the East circulated readily in the West, and their deficiencies in regard to Spanish history called for rectification. The first genuine Spanish–Arabic history known to us has been preserved only in an early Spanish recension, known as the *Chronica del Moro Rasis*. Most of the other early histories survive only in part, but a few precious volumes have been recovered of the major chronicle by one of the greatest of Muslim historians, Ibn Ḥayyān (987–1075). On the other hand, an important series of biographical works, beginning with the end of the tenth century and continuing into the thirteenth, has fortunately been preserved, and enables us to reconstruct in faithful detail the vigorous life of those literary circles that in their day represented the highest culture in Europe.

6

THE SILVER AGE

(A.D. 1055–1258)

ARABIC literature, as we have seen, was through its dependence on patronage very closely affected by the vicissitudes of Muslim history, and it is no arbitrary determination that fixes the turning-point in A.D. 1055. In that year a Turkish dynasty, the Seljuks or Seljukids, finally consolidated Turkish hegemony in western Asia by entering Baghdād. Along with and after them a succession of nomadic Turkoman tribes established themselves in eastern and northern Persia, Adharbaijan, northern Syria, and Anatolia. The sultans with their slave armies strove in vain to maintain some sort of stability against the nomads and the ambitions of their own generals. With rare exceptions the history of their rule in Asia is one of constant revolts and political anarchy, with all their attendant evils of devastation, depopulation, and fiscal exactions. It will readily be conceived how unfavourable such conditions were to the maintenance, not merely of literature, but of any form of culture. The occasional advent of a strong and enlightened ruler or series of rulers could not materially improve the situation, as in the course of two centuries the armatures of civil government and economic prosperity built up by the Arabs and Persians were relentlessly weakened or destroyed in province after province.

In another respect also the rise of Turkish dynasties adversely affected Arabic literature. The Persian princes had all been familiar with Arabic and were able to exercise a discriminating patronage. But the Turks who ruled in western Asia were rarely versed in Arabic, and it was in their time that Persian re-established its literary predominance. Not only did this siphon off into Persian literature the talents which might otherwise have rejuvenated Arabic literature or opened it up to new experiences, but it narrowed down the field of royal patronage. Arabic works gained a hearing only at second hand, and the favour of the Turkish rulers was largely determined by the Arabic-speaking personnel of the court, who were in most cases theologians or secretaries. As the former were opposed to independent thought on principle and the latter were rarely interested in anything outside philology in its various literary elaborations, the obstacles placed in the way of a writer whose works did not conform to their standards were wellnigh insurmountable. One result of this appears in the apologetic, even servile, tone which, although found in Arabic literature from the earliest times, becomes increasingly prominent. It is a curious exercise to read the pleas which writers of non-theological works found it necessary to insert in their prefaces.

I am well aware [says Yāqūt in his *Dictionary of Learned Men*] of odious critics who will revile and disparage me, men whose mind has been poisoned by ignorance and whose inmost soul revolts against generous gifts of nature, declaring that it is of more importance to devote oneself to matters of religion and more useful in this world and the next. Do they not know that men are fashioned in different moulds and with different capacities? God has appointed for every science men to preserve it in its completeness and bring order into its substance, and every man is guided to that for which he was created. I do not deny that if I were to cleave to my mosque and my prayer-mat such conduct would be better adapted to the path of safety in the future life. But to pursue the best has been denied to me, and surely it suffices to a man for virtue that he does nothing reprehensible and walks not in the way of deceit.

In the Arabic-speaking lands, of course, the conditions were relatively more favourable; during the first of the two centuries covered in this chapter, Baghdād retained an almost undisputed primacy in western Asia, but in the second Syria and Egypt were beginning to rival it in their output of works of literature.

Apart from the external political factors, however, there were other forces which in both regions contributed to a growing deterioration in the quality, in spite of the marked increase in quantity, of the works produced from now onwards. As the literary circle narrowed down to a highly educated minority, its mind and literary standards narrowed in keeping and, as always happens, sought to compensate for loss of range and vitality by pedantry and affectation. Independence of thought gave place to reliance on authority; original works were superseded by the popular compendium, or the encyclopaedia. The elegance and artistry that clothed the inventive productions of bygone writers with grace and wit were now cultivated for themselves and smothered the matter, as if to hide the essential dullness of mind of the age; in Montaigne's phrase, they leapt on horseback because they lacked strength in their legs to march on foot. It must be remembered, too, how the richest growth of Arabic literature resulted from the contact of the native sciences with Greek thought. By now the Greek impetus was almost worked out, while the studies in which it was still the chief dynamic were discouraged and confined to a rapidly decreasing circle. The rigid scholasticism already prevalent in theology was symptomatic (but neither directly the cause nor the result) of the creeping paralysis which was affecting the mind of Islam.

It was during our present period that these influences, proceeding from the East, successfully permeated the whole fabric of Muslim culture. There can be little doubt that one factor which powerfully contributed to this success was the foundation of the great orthodox universities, of which the Niẓāmīya at Baghdād is the most famous. The chief task to which the young student was set was memory-training. Boys of six and seven memorized the Koran, the *Maqāmāt*, and the poetry of Mutanabbi. For years their entire activity by day and night was devoted to memorizing and studying enormous commentaries and super-commentaries on works of grammar, logic, and theology. It can have been no uncommon thing for a student in his twenties to carry between one and two hundred prose works in his head. By their control of higher education the theologians were able to sterilize all but genius and to eliminate the dangers arising from too independent a temperament and range of study. Such suppression, however, exacts its own penalty, and it is perhaps not wholly paradoxical that it is precisely in the sphere of theology that the original thought of the age found its chief field of activity.

§ 1. IRAQ AND PERSIA

It is with the greatest figure in Muslim religious thought that the period opens. Al-Ghazālī (1059–1111), after a brilliant career at Nīshāpūr and Baghdād, suddenly renounced his professorship and for ten years withdrew from the world. He himself tells us that his mind gave way under the strain of scepticism, and he felt that he must set himself to regain the faith he had lost. In scholastic theology, in philosophy, in the Shiʿite doctrines, he found no satisfaction. At length he turned to Ṣūfism and the light broke upon him. Returning to his native town of Ṭūs he spent the remaining years of his life in study and contemplation with his disciples.

His literary activities began while he was yet a professor at Baghdād with a number of treatises designed to counteract the heresies opposed to Sunnī orthodoxy. First he underpinned the dogmatic positions of Sunnism by a sustained logical argument. Then the esoteric doctrines of the extreme Shiʿites were demolished in a powerful polemic. Next came the turn of the philosophers; in **The Incoherence of the Philosophers* the arguments of Avicenna were criticized with vigour and acumen, but its object was not so much to demolish philosophy as to bind it to the service of theology by combating the exclusive use of reason. It was, however, the series of works he wrote after his conversion to the Ṣūfī life that mark an era in Islam. His aim in these was to bring the inner light of Ṣūfism into orthodox theology to redress the balance lost by the excessive scholasticism of the Ashʿarite school, to substitute subjective religious experience for 'systems and classifications, words and arguments about words'. In the **Rescuer from Error* (*Munqidh*) he illustrates by his own experience the grounds of his faith, which was expounded in full in his chief work **Iḥyā' ʿUlūm ad-Dīn* ('The Revivification of the Religious Sciences'). Besides these standard works, he wrote for popular use a number of devotional treatises both in Arabic and Persian, some of which bear a striking resemblance in tone and matter to evangelical tracts of our own time.

Ghazālī was not so much an original thinker as a man of intense personality. The immediate effect of his work was to leaven the orthodox church with the moral vigour of the best elements in Ṣūfism. But for all that he was too far above his age, and his revolt against the ethics of the scholastics too radical. To later generations he was no more than one of many theologians; the *Iḥyā* was neglected, and it was not until it was reintroduced at the end of the eighteenth century that the Muslim world began to awake to his significance. For European students he has long held a peculiar fascination, and like his great opponent Ibn Rushd (p. 137) is one of the few figures in Muslim history round whom a large European literature has arisen.

We shall appreciate better the revolutionary nature of Ghazālī's work if we contrast with him two famous theologians of the time. Az-Zamakhsharī of Khwārizm (1075–1143) belonged to the philological school of theology; few books used to be better known in the Arabic schools of Europe than his handbook of grammar (*al-Mufaṣṣal*) and the collection of moral apophthegms in polished rhymed prose called **The Golden Necklaces*. Fakhr ad-Dīn ar-Rāzī (1149–1209), on the other hand, was a philosopher and encyclopaedist and one of the greatest humanists of his time. He is said to have been the first to employ a systematic arrangement in his writings, which ranged from philosophy and theology to talismans and astrology. Both, however, are famed chiefly for their Commentaries on the Koran, the writing of which seems to have been a frequent exercise at the time.

> All sorts of erudite persons [says Suyūṭī] took to compiling commentaries, but every one of them confined himself to his

own special science. The grammarian, you will see, has no eyes for anything but grammatical constructions and the number of ways in which the words can be taken; the historian interests himself in nothing but the narrative sections—these he expands in minutest detail—and in stories of the ancients, whether they be true or false; the legist makes of his an almost unending discourse on law and goes out of his way to establish proofs of legal points out of verses which have not the slightest concern with anything of the sort; while the exponent of the intellectual sciences, especially the Imām Fakhr ad-Dīn, fills his with sayings of the Muslim and Greek philosophers, deducing one thing from another until the reader is lost in amazement at the incongruity of the final doctrine with the original verse, so that a learned theologian said of it, 'It contains everything but the commentary'.

Though Zamakhsharī held the Muʿtazilite heresy, his commentary, entitled *The Unveiler*, obtained so wide a vogue that a century later its sting was drawn in an expurgated edition by al-Baiḍāwī (d. 1286) and in this form it remains to this day the most popular commentary.

In the domain of philology and belles-lettres proper, all other names during this period are overshadowed by that of al-Ḥarīrī of Baṣra (1054–1122). He received the usual philological education in the still famous school of his native town and filled a minor post in the bureaucracy, which with a small inheritance enabled him to pursue his philological studies. Like most men of his class since the time of Badīʿ az-Zamān, he had acquired a ready mastery over the art of *sajʿ*, but had not apparently written anything of note until he sprang suddenly into fame by the publication of his **Maqāmāt*. These were frankly imitated from Badīʿ az-Zamān, the imitation extending not only to the literary form but even to the *mise en scéne* and the character of the narrators, Ḥarīrī's Abu Zayd of Sarūj being represented as just such another witty vagabond as Hamadhānī's Abu'l-Fatḥ of Alexandria. The incident which led him to compose his *Maqāmāt* is thus related in his own words:

Abū Zayd of Sarūj was an importunate old beggar, full of eloquence, who came to us in Baṣra and one day stood up in the mosque of the Banū Ḥarām (the quarter in which Ḥarīrī lived) and after pronouncing a greeting begged alms of the people. Some of the magistrates were present, the mosque being crammed with eminent men, and they were charmed with his eloquence and wit and the beautiful phrasing of his speech. On this occasion he related the capture of his daughter by the Greeks, as I have related it in the Maqāma called 'Of the Ḥarām'. That same evening a number of the eminent and learned men of Baṣra were gathered at my house and I told them what I had seen and heard of this beggar and of the elegant style and witty allusiveness which he had employed to effect his purpose. Thereupon every one else there told how he too had seen of this same beggar, each in his own mosque, what I had seen, and how he had heard him deliver on other subjects a discourse even better than the one I had heard, for he used to change his dress and appearance in every mosque and show his skill in all kinds of artifices. They were astonished at the pains he took to gain his object and at his cunning in changing his appearance and at his ingenuity. So I wrote the 'Maqāma of the Ḥarām' and thereafter constructed upon it the remainder of the Maqāmāt.[1]

From the very first Ḥarīrī's *Maqāmāt* were regarded as incomparable. 'Had he claimed them as a miracle', says

[1] From Yāqūt's *Irshād*. For the history of the composition of the remaining *Maqāmāt* and of Ḥarīrī's mortification and final triumph, the reader may be referred to the introduction prefixed by Thomas Chenery to his annotated translation of the first twenty-six *Maqāmāt* (there are fifty in all), a work which holds a place in the first rank of European translations from the Arabic.

one biographer, 'not one would have been found to reject the claim.' It is chiefly for their literary and linguistic qualities that they are prized, but the infinite allusions to all branches of learning and all sides of life have rendered them a monument of erudition. Nor is it merely their formal perfection, the mastery of language, the endless *tours de force* and cunning obscurities that have gained for them their privileged position. Ḥarīrī has had many successors whose linguistic attainments, though perhaps little inferior to his, have not preserved their work from oblivion. But Ḥarīrī never forgot that the primary purpose of the *Maqāmāt* was to amuse and entertain, and throughout his book the wit of the descriptions and the dialogue is set off by the delicacy and charm of the verses and the more serious passages.

For more than seven centuries [says Chenery] his work has been esteemed as, next to the Koran, the chief treasure of the Arabic tongue. Contemporaries and posterity have vied in praise of him. His assemblies have been commented on with infinite learning and labour in Andalusia, and on the banks of the Oxus. To appreciate his marvellous eloquence, to fathom his profound learning, to understand his varied and endless allusions, have always been the highest object of the literary, not only among the Arabic-speaking peoples, but wherever the Arabic language has been scientifically studied.

Moreover, Ḥarīrī's *Maqāmāt*, like those of Hamadhānī, possess an inner vitality from the fact that they are firmly rooted in the common life of the Islamic city, and portray its manners and its humours so realistically as to constitute one of the most precious social documents of the medieval civilization. It is not surprising that this was one of the few works of Arabic belles-lettres to be decorated with miniatures, a few specimens of which have survived to our time.

Few of the other Arabic works written in the East during this period are of special interest to us. The arts of rhetoric and euphuism were reduced to textbook form by as-Śakkākī of Khwārizm (d. 1229) in *The Key to the Sciences*, which enjoys the distinction of being probably the most frequently and widely abstracted, glossed, and commented on of all secular works in Arabic. Persian was gradually coming into its own as the language of poetry; only one Arabic ode, the peevish **L-poem of the Foreigners* of aṭ-Ṭughrāʿī (d. *c.* 1121), has won a place in literary history, and that probably less by its sterling qualities than because of its author's wit in linking its name with Shanfarā's famous ode (p. 28). In the field of history, the Sunnī revival encouraged a revival of the Islamic 'universal history'; the first of these, devoted more to biography than to political history, was apparently the chronicle of the Ḥanbalite preacher Ibn al-Jauzī (d. 1200), who introduced also a new type of homiletic *adab* and vigorously satirized the Ṣūfīs in **The Deceits of the Devil.* But the secretarial type of dynastic history still continued to be cultivated, its last Arabic representative in the East being a *biography of the last Sultan of Khwārizm, written in 1241 by his secretary an-Nasawī. Two other writers, however, stand out above their fellows, and one of them was a Greek.

It was probably by Ibn Ḥazm's work (p. 115) that the theologian and philosopher ash-Shahristānī (1086–1153) was inspired to write a similar **Book of Religious and Philosophical Sects*, than which there are few works in Arabic literature that reflect more credit on medieval Muhammadan scholarship. Shahristānī was a man of cultured tastes and wide tolerance, whose interest in philosophical heresies was incomprehensible to his contemporaries. His book includes accounts not only of the Muslim sects and philosophical schools, but also of the various Jewish schools and Christian churches, the Greek philosophers from Thales downwards, and the early Christian fathers, and even of the Indian religious philosophies. Himself strictly orthodox, he presents the arguments and views of even the most heretical schools with remarkable fairness, only occasionally interposing an incisive comment at the end of some peculiarly obnoxious or hair-splitting doctrine.

Yāqūt (*c.* 1179–1229) ranks among the most successful of Arabic compilers. By birth an Anatolian Greek, he was enslaved in boyhood, educated as a Muslim, and employed by his master, a merchant of Baghdād, as a travelling clerk, in which capacity he made several journeys to Syria, Persia, and the Persian Gulf. On gaining his liberty he earned a livelihood by copying and selling manuscripts, and was attracted to Merv by its magnificent libraries. Fleeing from the East before the Mongols in 1220, he reached Mosul in a state of utter destitution and there began his work a second time, removing finally to Aleppo. His **Geographical Dictionary* or Gazetteer is not only the most important work of Arabic geography of its kind, but includes also brief historical notices of the provinces and more important cities, and biographical data on many personages connected with them. Such a work, however useful, could scarcely avoid a certain aridity, yet in Yāqūt's hands, by an anecdote or extract from a poem, a description of natural beauties, or some personal or literary reminiscence, it is astonishingly enlivened and enriched.

The same felicitous touch is found also in his *Dictionary*

of Men of Letters (*Irshād*), which has only recently come to light again, though it was apparently more highly esteemed by his contemporaries than his other works. It is a work of the first importance for the history of Arabic literature, and, as the passages on al-Bīrūnī, Ḥarīrī, and others quoted above show, abounds with interesting anecdotes and extracts. Ibn Khallikān (p. 133) inserts in his biographical notice of Yāqūt a long (though to western taste over-elaborate) letter addressed to his patron at Aleppo, describing his life in Khurāsān and his misfortunes after the Mongol invasion, which is of interest as a specimen of the later Persian–Arabic epistolary style.

§ 2. EGYPT AND SYRIA

In the last quarter of the twelfth century Syria was detached from the heretical Fāṭimids of Egypt and laid open to the influence of the Sunnī revival in the East. The long struggle during that century against the Crusaders stimulated a few *local chronicles and, a little later, a considerable output of books on military tactics and weapons, horsemanship, and the Holy War in general. But the most vivid work that it produced is the *autobiography of the Arab knight Usāma ibn Munqidh (1095–1188), a gallery of brilliant and revealing vignettes of the age. With the reunion of Syria and Egypt under Saladin and his successors, and the frustration of the Third Crusade, there opened for both countries a new era of prosperity which was reflected in an outburst of literary activity, especially in the domains of poetry and history.

Neither Syria nor Egypt, of course, had at any time lacked poets of local reputation. The stimulus which now raised for a time the level of poetic art was the introduction of Ṣūfī mysticism, together with a backwash of influences from Spain, including the *muwashshaḥ*. It was the famous Spanish–Arab mystic Ibn ʿArabī of Murcia (1165–1240) who, it is said, gave the *muwashshaḥ* an established position in eastern poetry. Ibn ʿArabī was not indeed primarily a poet. His chief mystical and didactic work, *The Meccan Revelations*, and most of his other writings are in prose, but his great reputation gained for his poems (the best known of which is the collection called **The Interpreter of the* [*Soul's*] *Longings*) a wide circulation. In his poetry he carried to extremes the symbolism of the Ṣūfīs in clothing mystical experiences in the language of human passion. That European students have often in consequence been misled (in spite of our familiarity with this symbolism in such Persian poets as Ḥāfiẓ) is not surprising, for even Muslim critics have expressed grave doubts of the genuineness of the mystical interpretation claimed for them.

Surpassing Ibn ʿArabi in poetic gift, and universally acclaimed as the greatest Arabic mystic poet and the only one who can challenge the great Persian mystics, was his contemporary *ʿOmar ibn al-Fāriḍ (1181–1235). Like all of these, he clothes his experiences in the language of human love, yet throughout

> God is the Beloved whom the poet addresses and celebrates under many names—now as one of the heroines of Arabian minne-song, now as a gazelle or a driver of camels, or as an archer shooting deadly glances from his eye; most frequently as plain He or She. The Odes retain the form, conventions, topics, and images of ordinary love-poetry; their inner meaning hardly ever obtrudes itself, although its presence is everywhere suggested by a strange exaltation of feeling.[1]

Nor is it only in outward construction that Ibn al-Fāriḍ's

[1] R. A. Nicholson, *Studies in Islamic Mysticism* (Cambridge, 1921).

art is linked to the traditional Arabic poetry; the rhetorical set of his phraseology, the conceits and word-plays and *tours de force* all follow closely the fashion set by Mutanabbī. Of his *dīwān*, a slender volume, scarcely exceeding twenty odes with other shorter pieces, the best known poems are the oft-translated *Wine-Song* and the long *Mystic's Progress*, a didactic poem of 760 lines describing his own mystical experience, which ranks as the crowning achievement of Arabic mystical poetry. The following fragment describing the vision of Divine beauty (from one of his lesser odes) displays, in R. A. Nicholson's translation, the charm of his language:

> Though he be gone, mine every limb beholds him
> In every charm and grace and loveliness:
> In music of the lute and flowing reed
> Mingled in consort with melodious airs;
> And in green hollows where in cool of eve
> Gazelles roam browsing, or at break of morn;
> And where the gathered clouds let fall their rain
> Upon a flowery carpet woven of blooms;
> And where at dawn with softly-trailing skirts
> The zephyr brings to me his balm most sweet;
> And when in kisses from the flagon's mouth
> I suck wine-dew beneath a pleasant shade.

Even among the minor and more mundane poets there was a temporary recovery from the subservience of matter to style which for two centuries had been crushing the life out of Arabic poetry. Bahā' ad-Dīn Zuhair 'of Egypt' (d. 1258) is the best known of the court poets of the time. His **dīwān* is marked by simplicity of language, absence of flunkery, and genuine depth of feeling, which with a delicate play of fancy give his poems something of a western flavour, and led his English translator[1] to compare him to Herrick.

On a Blind Girl

They called my love a poor blind maid:
I love her more for that, I said;
I love her, for she cannot see
These gray hairs which disfigure me.
We wonder not that wounds are made
By an unsheathed and naked blade;
The marvel is that swords should slay,
While yet within their sheaths they stay.
She is a garden fair, where I
Need fear no guardian's prying eye;
Where, though in beauty blooms the rose,
Narcissuses their eyelids close.

Saladin's career naturally formed the subject of several biographies, the two earliest of which were written by men who had served under him. 'Imād ad-Dīn, generally known as 'The Secretary from Iṣfahān' (1125–1201), came to Damascus after service in Iraq, subsequently joined Saladin as personal secretary, and accompanied him on all his campaigns. His first historical work on the Seljuks of Iraq survives only in an abridgement, and of his semi-autobiographical work on the career of Saladin only two out of seven volumes are known to exist, besides a shorter book on the reconquest of Jerusalem and the Third Crusade. He and his official superior, al-Qāḍī al-Fāḍil (d. 1200), Saladin's chief secretary, were the most celebrated stylists of the century, and it is not surprising that he exerted all his powers of ornate prose to do justice to the epic quality of Saladin's achievement. Nevertheless,

[1] E. H. Palmer, *Dīwān of Bahā ad-Dīn Zuhayr* (Cambridge, 1877), from which the following verses are quoted.

his works, together with the abridgement made by *Abū Shāma of Damascus (d. 1268), remain a first-rate source, and are complemented by the less elaborate, more intimate, and movingly sincere biography of Saladin by his military judge, *Bahā' ad-Dīn of Moṣul (d. 1234), for the period of the Third Crusade.

A third contemporary account of Saladin is less friendly to him. Ibn al-Athīr (1160–1234), an Arab by birth, ranks among the greatest Arabic historians. His earlier work, a **History of the Atabegs of Moṣul*, finished in 1211, is devoted to Saladin's chief Muslim opponents and naturally tends to disparage Saladin's achievements in favour of the historian's own patrons. The scales are somewhat more evenly held in his greater work, **al-Kāmil* ('The Perfection of History'). An extensive work in twelve volumes, it contains a universal history of Islam down to his own times, excerpted from the works of former historians; for the first three centuries it is little more than an abridgement of Ṭabarī's great work (which was over-elaborate for later students) with additions from other sources. Its value lies not only in the extracts from works now lost, but also in the more flexible handling of his materials and less static sense of history than is usual among Muslim historians. Although it became the standard source for later Muslim compilers, it is a curious fact that it remained unknown until the nineteenth century, and that all earlier orientalists, Gibbon's authorities included, were forced to rely on its imitations and abridgements by the Copt *al-Makīn (1205–73) and the gifted Sultan of Ḥamāh, *Abu'l-Fidā (1273–1331).

Almost all the other works of general interest of this time are also more or less related to history. The **Description of Egypt* by ʿAbd al-Laṭīf of Baghdād (1160–1231), a physician and writer of encyclopaedic range, is, however, one of the most original scientific treatises in Arabic. Besides a full description of its flora, fauna, and ancient monuments (including a first-hand narrative of an attempt to pull down the Pyramids), it contains a gruesome account of the outbreak of cannibalism in Cairo during the great famine of 1200–1, and throws some interesting sidelights on the medical studies of the time.

Far more celebrated, both in Europe and the East, is the *Biographical Dictionary (*The Obituaries of Eminent Men*) of Ibn Khallikān (1211–82), of Syrian birth, but claiming descent from the famous Bactrian family of the Barmakids. While still in his teens he had studied at Aleppo just after the death of Yāqūt, and it may have been from Yāqūt's biographical dictionary that he conceived the idea of compiling a similar work on wider lines. Instead of confining himself to a particular class of writers he included in his scheme men of eminence in every branch of life, omitting only the first and second generations of Muslims and the caliphs, of whom abundant biographies already existed (Ibn al-Athīr, for instance, compiled a biographical work on 7,500 'Companions' of the Prophet, under the allusive title of *Lions of the Thicket*). In his endeavour to attain the utmost accuracy he even omitted all persons of the date of whose death he could not find reliable information. His style is free from the straining after rhetorical effect that disfigures so much later literature, and in addition to many extracts from works now lost, the anecdotes with which the book is enlivened and the miscellaneous information incidentally conveyed make it not only most entertaining to read, but also one of the most valuable mirrors of medieval Muslim life.[1]

[1] A selection from de Slane's excellent annotated translation has

The encyclopaedic works of Yāqūt, Ibn Khallikān, and Ibn al-Athīr exemplify a trend towards compilation, which is almost certainly to be related to the growth of scholasticism and was in later centuries to replace original composition more and more in scholarship and literary activity. We have good reason, however, to be grateful for such biographical dictionaries of men of science as those of al-Qifṭī (d. 1248) and Ibn Abī Uṣaibiʿa (d. 1270), which are our most precious sources for the history of science and medicine in the high noon of the Islamic civilization. Two other biographical dictionaries, the *History of Damascus* of Ibn ʿAsākir (d. 1176) and the biographical supplement to the *History of Aleppo* by Ibn al-ʿAdīm (d. 1262), were planned and carried out on such a massive scale that the first has only been partially edited, and nobody has yet attempted to publish the second.

§ 3. SICILY

For over two centuries, from the middle of the ninth till the latter part of the eleventh, Sicily, under the turbulent rule of Arab chieftains, formed a part of the Muslim world and produced a number of Arabic philologists and poets. Of the latter, whose verse bears evident traces of Spanish influence, the most famous is Ibn Ḥamdīs (*c.* 1055–1132). Like many of his fellow countrymen, he fled the island at the Norman conquest and took refuge with Muʿtamid (p. 112) at Seville, where much of his best poetry was written. He accompanied Muʿtamid into exile in Morocco, and on his death returned to Tunisia. The love of nature displayed in his work has gained for him the name of 'The Arabic Wordsworth'.

been made by Mr. E. V. Lucas in his amusing essay entitled *A Boswell of Baghdad*.

It was only after the Norman re-conquest of the island, however, that the Saracen genius of Sicily reached its full fruition in the rich outburst of Arabo-Norman art and culture. For a century Sicily furnishes the unique spectacle of a Christian kingdom in which Saracens not only were tolerated but occupied high positions, and Arabic was one of the languages of the court. Few contemporary Muslim rulers equalled the Sicilian Normans in their patronage of Arabic letters, and few found a worthier client than did Roger II in the Sharīf Idrīsī (1099– ?). After studying in Spain and much travel in western lands Idrīsī was invited by Roger to settle at Palermo as a sort of geographer-royal, and with the assistance of the prince, who collected information from observers in different countries, compiled in 1154 his famous geographical treatise **The Pleasure of the Ardent Enquirer*, more commonly called *The Book of Roger*, a work which in competent opinion bears comparison with Strabo, though the author shows himself more credulous than his eastern predecessors such as Maqdisī.

Shortly after 1154 another Sicilian exile, Ibn Ẓafar (d. 1169), during a brief return to his native land, dedicated to one of the Arab governors a book of essays under the title of **Consolation Philtres for the Man of Authority*. The essays, which are devoted to the virtues of resignation, patience, and so forth, consist as usual in expositions of texts from Koran and Tradition, verses, and historical anecdotes. A more original feature is that the latter, though based on incidents of Arabic and Persian history, are elaborated by the introduction of fictitious characters (evidently modelled on the popular *Kalīla wa-Dimna*), and consequently deserve more properly the name of historical novelettes. Ibn Ẓafar wrote also a number of other works of belles-lettres, amongst them a book on remarkable children, still preserved in Paris.

§ 4. SPAIN

The part played by the Turks in the East was filled in the West by the Berbers. Under the bigoted rule of a new Berber dynasty, the Almorávids, which had taken advantage of the weakness of the petty states of Arab Spain to impose its rule over Andalusia in 1091, the fine flower of literature wilted, and the anthologists of this period perhaps did better service to Andalusian poetry than the contemporary poets. In the twelfth century, however, there appeared alongside the *muwashshaḥ* a second form of strophic verse, the *zajal* ('melody'), composed mainly in the popular speech and with no artificial refinements of construction. Practically its only literary representative is *Ibn Quzmān (d. 1159), the type of Muslim troubadour, living on the generosity of his patrons as he wandered from court to court. In the eastern Muslim lands the *zajal* never became popular; in the West, however, issuing from and appealing to the people, and spread by oral transmission, it may well have contributed (although the matter is much disputed) to the development and spread of vernacular poetry in Catalonia, Provence, and even Italy.

Half-way through the twelfth century, the Almorávids were overthrown by a second Berber dynasty, the Almóhads, under the influence of a remarkable theologian of the school of al-Ghazālī, Ibn Tūmart (d. 1130). The new rulers showed a much more tolerant attitude to letters, and in the latter half of the century there was a fresh burst of literary activity in Spain.

The most prominent figures in the new movement were philosophers, whose influence extended far beyond the bounds of Spain, and probably affected European thought far more deeply than that of their Muslim co-religionists. The first of the Spanish school of philosophy, Ibn Bāja (Avempace), belongs rather to the pre-Berber period, though he died in Morocco in 1138. He was followed by Ibn Ṭufail (d. 1185), whose fame rests chiefly on his revision of the philosophical romance composed by Avicenna, called **Ḥayy ibn Yaqẓān* ('The Living One, Son of the Waking One'), depicting the development of the mind of an island recluse by its own innate and uncorrupted powers to the highest philosophical level and the vision of the Divine. The mystic trend of the work is unmistakable, as in many of the Muslim philosophers. To assert as boldly as possible the rights of human reason, on the other hand, was the aim of Ibn Rushd (1126–98), who in reviving the study of Aristotle lent his name, barbarized as Averroes, as a battle-cry to the first assailants on the medieval Catholic philosophy in Europe. His chief work was undoubtedly his *commentaries on Aristotle, but to the Muslim world in general there was more interest in his vigorous criticism of and reply to Ghazālī's polemical work against the philosophers (p. 121), which he called **The Incoherence of the Incoherence*, and a *series of tractates on the relations between religion and philosophy. After an introductory argument that since the Koran frequently enjoins on men the study of the phenomena of Nature and this study involves the use of reason, it follows logically that the reason must be trained to the highest possible degree, he develops in these his audacious claim that any conflict between philosophic truth and revealed truth is to be resolved by allegorical interpretation of the latter, and that it must be open to philosophers (though not to the uneducated masses) so to interpret them and teach their meaning to the uneducated, i.e. the theologians. Renan, as is well known, regarded him in consequence as an absolute rationalist, but more recent students are inclined to modify this judgement. The last of the Spanish school, indeed the last of the Arab philosophers, was Ibn Sab'īn of Murcia (d. 1269), best known for his *correspondence (though its authenticity has been doubted) on philosophical subjects with the Emperor Frederick II. He was perhaps less a philosopher than a mystic, and his contemporaries described him as 'a Ṣūfī after the manner of the philosophers'.

History in this period is represented mainly by the continuing series of biographical works. The major figure in Andalusian letters in the thirteenth century, however, the versatile Ibn Sa'īd (d. 1274), was almost equally distinguished as poet, historian, geographer, and belle-lettrist, although his chronicle has been only partly preserved. He compiled also an *anthology, which his Spanish translator has called 'the last testament of Arabo-Andalusian poetry'.

The sense of remoteness from their ancestral lands in the East, from which they were separated by the long (and since the invasion of north Africa by Arab tribesmen vastly more dangerous) overland journey, was somewhat lessened for the Andalusian Arabs in the twelfth century by the expansion of sea communications between the western and eastern Mediterranean basins, a curious by-product of the Crusades. Muslims often, and apparently without difficulty, took passage on Christian ships plying to and from Syria and Egypt. We know of many instances of Andalusian travellers to the East, although few were as adventurous as Abū Ḥāmid of Granada (d. 1170), who went on to spend seven years in Hungary and eastern Europe. The commonest incentive to travel was, of course, the Pilgrimage to Mecca, and out of this came one of the most famous of Andalusian travel-books. The poet and traditionist Ibn Jubair of Valencia (1145–1217), during his first pilgrimage between 1183 and 1185, kept a *journal, which he published soon after his return to Granada, partly for the guidance of future Ḥājjīs. Apart from the liveliness of the narrative, the detailed descriptions of the cities of Egypt, the Ḥijāz, and Syria gained for the book a certain authority, not only in the West, where it was frequently quoted with or without acknowledgement by later travellers, but also in the East, largely on account of the extracts from it inserted by Ibn Jubair's own pupil ash-Sharīshī (i.e. the man from Xeres) in his standard commentary on the *Maqāmāt* of Ḥarīrī. Though the most valuable part for us is his full account of the ceremonies observed during the Pilgrimage at Mecca, this section does not lend itself to quotation, and the following description of a storm at sea is more typical of his style.

Early on the Tuesday night a wind sprang up, as the result of which the sea became agitated, accompanied by rain which the wind drove with such force that it resembled showers of arrows. We were in pitiful case and exceeding anxiety, for the waves beat on us from every side like moving mountains. All that night we spent in prey to despair, hoping that in the morning our distress would be alleviated, but the day brought a tempest yet more terrible and grievous; the swelling of the sea increased, the sky lowered in ashen blackness, and the wind and rain blew with such violence that no sail could hold fast against it. So recourse was had to small sails, but the wind seized one of these and tore it to shreds and broke the mast to which the sails are attached. Thereupon despair fastened on all hearts and the hands of the Muslims were lifted in prayer to God. So we abode the whole day, and when night fell the storm eased somewhat, we continuing on our journey all the while scudding under bare poles. We passed the night in alternations of hope and despair, but when the dawn broke God sent forth His mercy, the clouds dispersed, the air cleared, the sun shone, the sea began to subside, the people rejoiced, sociability returned and despair departed—praise be to God Who hath shown us the might of His power!

7

THE AGE OF THE MAMLŪKS

(A.D. 1258–1800)

THE successive blows by which the Mongols hewed their way across western Asia, culminating in the sack of Baghdād and the tragic extinction of the independent Caliphate in 1258, scarcely did more than give finality to a situation that had long been developing. The eastern Muslim world was split into separate and gradually diverging cultural areas. In Persia a new and brilliant literature arose from the ashes of the old civilization, but it was entirely Persian in language and feeling, and its offshoots in the new dominions in Anatolia and northern India developed in time their own characteristic Turkish and Indian features. Henceforth Egypt, emerging victoriously from the double struggle with the Mongols and Crusaders, is (with its dependency Syria) sole heir of the Arabic literature of the East. Even in Iraq, Arabic culture is represented only by a poet or two, some local chronicles, and the popular, but rather elementary, compendium of political ethics and Islamic history known as **al-Fakhrī*. Theological and legal works, of course, continued to be written chiefly in Arabic, but these branches had long since lost the right to a place in literary history. The decay of Arabic studies is vividly presented by the traveller Ibn Baṭṭūṭa. On visiting Baṣra in 1327, he tells us:

I attended once the Friday prayers at the Mosque, and when the preacher rose to deliver his sermon, he committed many serious grammatical errors. I was astonished at this and spoke of it to the qāḍī, who answered, 'In this town there is not one left who knows anything about grammar'. Here indeed is a warning for men to reflect on—Magnified be He who changes all things and overturns all human affairs! This Baṣra, in whose people the mastery of grammar reached its height, whence it had its origin and where it developed, which was the home of its leader [Sībawaih] whose preeminence is undisputed, has no preacher who can deliver a sermon without breaking its rules!

For the whole period of this chapter Egypt was governed by the Turkish and Circassian military caste called the Mamlūks ('White Slaves'). This space of five and a half centuries falls into two nearly equal divisions. Until 1517 the Mamlūks were independent rulers and Egypt, though troubled by incessant revolts, derived considerable material prosperity from the Indian trade; after the Ottoman conquest in that year a period sets in of universal stagnation and decay. As always, the political conditions were mirrored in literature; the output was enormous throughout, but the qualities of originality, virility, and imagination, weak from the first, die away completely by the sixteenth century.

§ 1. EGYPT AND SYRIA TO A.D. 1517

Only one poet of the Mamlūk age has gained any enduring reputation. The history of al-Būṣīrī (1212–*c.* 1296), who was of Berber extraction, is obscure; his name lives solely by virtue of his panegyric of the Prophet, called, in memory of his miraculous cure from paralysis by a vision that the Prophet cast his mantle (*burda*) over him, the **Burda* or *Mantle Ode*. It was at once received with admiration, which deepened into the veneration for its reputed miraculous power which it still retains, although in itself it has little title to such an outstanding position. In form a *qaṣīda*, it opens with the regulation *nasīb*, and leads into the main subject through a short didactic passage. Apart from its elegance and its general freedom from Ṣūfī ideas, from which it derives a certain pleasing simplicity, its chief interest to us is that it presents in brief compass the medieval legend of the Prophet.

Of the very extensive geographical literature of the time we may leave aside here the arm-chair geographers, who compiled bulky works from various written and oral sources; their near kinsmen the cosmographers, such as *Dimishqī (d. 1327), avid of marvels and rather sparing of sober fact; and the bald tabulations of scientific geographical data, like the celebrated *geography of Abu'l-Fidā (p. 132). On a different plane from these stand the manuals of the art of navigation for pilots and mariners on the Indian Ocean, which for convenience in memorizing were not uncommonly composed in iambic verse. A collection of such verses and a prose work on the same subject, written in 1489 by Ibn Mājid of Najd, the son of a famous pilot and himself a pilot of some distinction (it is claimed that it was he who piloted Vasco da Gama from Africa to the Indian coast), are only now coming to light for the first time, together with a number of similar treatises of slightly later date, dealing more especially with observation as a guide to latitudes. Another original feature is supplied by the minute topographical descriptions of Egypt, based on a cadastral survey and *Domesday Book* made in 1315. For general use these works were frequently abridged, as in the comprehensive manual for secretaries of al-Qalqashandī (d. 1418). After a long literary introduction and a discourse on the methods of writing and the technicalities to be observed in the matter of pen and ink, formulas, spacing, margins, and the like, the author inserts chapters on the geography of Egypt, *Syria, and other lands, both Muslim and non-Muslim, *the political and administrative organization of Egypt, courier-routes and pigeon-post stations, the calendars used by different peoples, specimens of the official correspondence carried on with foreign rulers and of other epistolary and documentary styles, the art of filing and précis-writing, and a host of other matters, to which we are indebted for many valuable sidelights on the Muslim world in the fourteenth century.

Even more than the preceding period of Arabic literature, its Byzantine age was marked by a vast output of encyclopaedic and biographical works. The most ambitious of the latter, an immense *History of Islām* by adh-Dhahabī (d. 1348) and an equally voluminous dictionary by aṣ-Ṣafadī (d. 1363), both only partially published as yet, aim at supplying comprehensive biographies for the whole of the first seven centuries, the first in a chronological framework, the second in alphabetical order. A novel method introduced by the historian Ibn Ḥajar (d. 1449) was to compile centennial dictionaries. For his own, a four-volume work on all notabilities who died in the eighth (fourteenth) century, he adopted a principle of selection so catholic as to include not only sultans, viziers, officials, military officers, scholars, saints, and poets, but also merchants, chess-players, and even one or two brigands. For the next century as-Sakhāwī (d. 1497) produced a twelve-volume dictionary, the twelfth volume of which is devoted to women. Among other encyclopaedic works the most notable are the fourteen-volume 'manual' of Qalqashandī already mentioned, and a zoological dictionary by ad-Damīrī (d. 1405), as much a work of letters as of natural science, and a mine of curious information.

Such encyclopaedic compilations cannot be denied a certain vitality of their own, but on the whole bear witness rather to industry than to imagination. Originality of mind, however, does break through, even if rarely, and interestingly enough just where it might least be expected, in half a dozen technical works in the long-stagnating fields of theology, law, and philology. The outstanding figure is the religious thinker and reformer, *Ibn Taimīya of Damascus (d. 1328), who stoutly braved sultan, doctors, and imprisonment in his hearty polemic against both the Ṣūfī cults and the inertia of the schools. It was not until the eighteenth century that he began to reap his reward, among the Wahhābīs of Arabia, and only in our own time has the measure of his stature come to be more widely appreciated.

The most impressive production of the Mamlūk age is concentrated in the field of history. Although the greatest historians of the period hailed from Persia and Tunis respectively,[1] no such sequence of conscientious historians is known to us as those of Syria and Egypt in the fourteenth and fifteenth centuries. Even to mention all their names and principal works would take us too long, and we must let one stand for all. While al-Maqrīzī (1346–1442) may be little more original or critical than his

[1] The Vizier Rashīd ad-Dīn (d. 1318), whose exhaustive history of the Mongols includes also summaries of the history of India, China, and Europe and was written in both Persian and Arabic, and Ibn Khaldūn (pp. 153–5 below.)

fellows, and no less unscrupulous in plundering earlier works without acknowledgement, he is distinguished by the breadth of his interests and the careful industry with which he collected and put in order enormous masses of historical and economic data. His aim seems to have been to compile a complete cycle of reference works on Egypt, and to this he devoted the last twenty years of his life. We possess from his hand an extremely detailed *topographical description of Egypt (known as the *Khiṭaṭ*), with special reference to its antiquities; a portion of a history of the Fāṭimid dynasty (*I'tibār*), the loss of the latter part of which is especially regrettable; a second history of the Ayyūbid and *Mamlūk dynasties (*Sulūk*), brought down to the year 1440; a few volumes of the original manuscript of an unfinished biographical dictionary of famous Egyptians, planned on a scale so vast that it is astonishing that any single individual should have undertaken to collect the material for it; and several monographs on historical subjects, including one on coinage.

One other Arabic historian has, in virtue of the subject of his biography, long enjoyed a reputation in Europe. Ibn 'Arabshāh (1392–1450) was born in Damascus and as a child removed by Tīmūr (Tamerlane) to Samarqand. We meet him later as secretary to the Ottoman Sultan at Adrianople, and finally engaged in literary pursuits in Damascus and Cairo. His biography of Tīmūr, entitled **The Marvels of Destiny*, is written in rhymed prose in the extremely ornate style, embellished with poetical quotations and all the flowers of rhetoric, which was favoured by Persian writers of the period, but in contrast to these and the earlier Arabic productions in rhymed prose breathes a spirit of bitter hostility to his hero. None of his other works has gained the same recognition; the best known is *The Entertainment of Caliphs*, a revision in the same style of an old north-Persian collection of tales.

The line of Mamlūk encyclopaedists closes appropriately, in the last half-century before the Ottoman conquest, with the greatest polygraph in Islam, Jalāl ad-Dīn as-Suyūṭī (i.e. of Assiut, 1445–1505). In Arabic literature, as we have seen, there is no lack of writers whose works run into three figures, yet for all that the tale of Suyūṭī's productions seems incredible. We possess the names of 561 works from his hand, and of these about 450 are known to be still in existence. Many, of course, are short treatises of a few pages, but not a few are bulky volumes. They range over the whole field of contemporary literary and scientific studies; some of them are merely collections of citations, as in his monographs on various minutiae of theological interest (e.g. how many persons constitute a congregation at Friday prayers), and some are original works in which the available materials are reorganized, often to advantage. The most important of these are: (1) a valuable treatise on the sciences connected with the Koran (*Itqān*, from which the quotation on page 122 has been taken); (2) and (3) a compendious commentary on the Koran and treatise on Arabic grammar; (4) a **History of the Caliphs*; (5) a handbook on the history, institutions, monuments, and notabilities of Egypt (including among the last a biography of himself). By their convenience, inclusiveness, and easy style, Suyūṭī's treatises soon gained an audience from one end of the Islamic world to the other, and have for nearly four centuries held an authoritative position as the interpreter and epitomizer of the Muslim classical tradition.

The decline of the classical literature was, as often happens, the opportunity for the language and literature of the people. Both in the East and the West popular poetry and popular romances began to receive more attention; even poems written in the popular speech made an appearance in circles to which hitherto they had been foreign. But the grip of tradition and the concentration of learning in the hands of the few strangled the attempt, and that so effectively that it can be said with a large measure of truth that no spoken dialect of Arabic has ever succeeded in becoming a literary medium. The popular literature, on the other hand, was rather grudgingly conceded a place; its productions were superficially adjusted to literary standards, and so there came into Arabic literature those story-cycles and romances of which one has gained for itself, under the title of *Arabian Nights*, a permanent place in the international literature of the world—often, it is to be feared, the only work of all the vast literature of Islam that is familiar to European ears. The early history of the compilation called the **Thousand and One Nights* is still obscure. The frame-story of Shahrāzād and Dīnārzād, which has been traced eventually to India, seems to have served as the standard framework for such collections (for example, that of the **Hundred and One Nights*) and it is fairly certain that, though the *Arabian Nights* began with a translation of an older Persian collection, new tales were gradually substituted for the earlier ones. There never was, in fact, until recently a clearly defined collection of tales recognized as forming the *Thousand and One Nights*. Different story-tellers made up the tale of nights with different materials, including folk-lore elements from the most diverse countries, and even the language of the manuscripts varies greatly in literary accuracy. The first European translation, that of Galland, was made from an earlier recension than the quite modern text now generally adopted, which omits two of the best known tales—those of 'Alī Bābā and of 'Alā' ad-Dīn (Aladdin). All the stories, however, from whatever source derived, have been as closely assimilated to Muslim ideas as the local Cairene tales; the entire work is a canvas to which the Arab mind has faithfully and indelibly, though unconsciously, transferred the image of itself.

In Arab lands the *Thousand and One Nights* has often been surpassed in popularity by the portentous romances, sometimes in prose only, more often in prose and verse, that have gathered round various historical or legendary persons or events. The best known is that of *'Antar, the slave-born poet-hero of the desert, which is almost equalled in popular favour by the Crusading romance that centres on the Mamlūk sultan Baybars. To the European reader (or listener, as these romances are read out at breakneck speed to a coffee-house audience) the constant repetition of similar incidents gives them rather a monotonous character, but the appeal which they make to the Arab is undeniable.

Yet another popular entertainment, the *Shadowgraph play, found in the oculist and wit Ibn Dāniyāl (d. 1310) a writer who attempted to give it a literary connexion. It would be interesting to speculate on the opportunity thus given to Arabic of developing a dramatic literature. But the opportunity was missed; except for this fleeting moment the shadowgraph remained in its rudimentary state, and Arabic drama was stillborn.

§ 2. SPAIN AND NORTH-WEST AFRICA

The overthrow of the Almóhad dynasty early in the thirteenth century and the re-conquest of Andalusia by the Christians, except for a narrow strip running from Gibraltar to Granada, was an event full of consequence for Spanish–Arabic literature. In the small remnant of its Spanish territories the Moorish civilization continued to exist for nearly three centuries with a splendour symbolized by the superb palace of its royal dynasty at Granada. We possess, it is true, few monuments of its literature, partly because of the loss of Muslim works after the reconquest by Ferdinand and Isabella, but one writer at least stands out above his contemporaries for sheer mastery of the craft of letters. Ibn al-Khaṭīb (1313–74), in the course of an adventurous political career, found time for an astonishing variety of literary activities. Of his works there are extant, in published texts or manuscripts, several collections of poems, letters, and documents, numerous historical works, monographs, and essays, of which those dealing with Granada possess the greatest interest for us. He had a taste for ornamental prose, which in his hands regains something of its earlier naturalness and elegance, and we must also apparently regard him as the last notable Andalusian poet and writer of *muwashshaḥs*, which seem to have died out in Spain by the end of the fourteenth century.

Of a very different order is the work entitled **The Ornament of Chevaliers and Banner of Gallants*, written to the Sultan's command by Ibn Hudhail of Granada about 1400, with the aim of encouraging the people of the province to take part in the Holy War against the Christians. The horse, as was to be expected, inspired a whole literature in Arabic, and Ibn Hudhail's book, which was based on earlier treatises now lost, treats fully of such subjects as its proportions, qualities, vices and gaits, saddlery, and the management of arms on horseback.

Under the pressure of the infidel, however, there was a steady emigration of Spanish families into the fringes of the opposite coast, and there is to be found the true continuation of Hispano-Muslim culture. In spite of political troubles and the general chaos in the interior, there persisted in Fez, Tlemsen, and the coast towns the old manners and the old love of letters of the great noble families of Andalusia. First Tunis in the thirteenth century and then Fez in the fourteenth rise into prominence as centres of Muslim civilization scarcely inferior at their height to the great eastern cities.

We must pass over the poets, the popular theologians, and the legists and grammarians in order to give adequate attention to the two most original figures of fourteenth-century Arabic literature. In 1325 Muḥammad Ibn Baṭṭūṭa (1304–77) set out from his native town of Tangier to make the pilgrimage to Mecca. The young man, already distinguished for his piety and learning, his curiosity whetted by the adventures of the journey, was led by degrees to form a resolve to visit every Muhammadan country and any others that opportunity offered. He collected interviews with crowned heads as later men have collected their autographs, and became in the process a personage of consequence, travelling with a large retinue from court to court. All the while he stored in a retentive memory notes on the various countries and their peoples, manners, products, and other details, and when, after travels extending to east Africa, Constantinople, and the Russian steppes, India, Ceylon, and China, he returned home in 1349, he rested only a few months before rounding them off by visits to Granada and the Negro Muslim lands on the Niger. His tales, as we know from Ibn Khaldūn, were received with some incredulity at Fez, where by the Sultan's command he dictated his travels to the scribe Ibn Juzayy, and his work appears to have been quite unknown to eastern writers. Some bald *summaries of it procured at the beginning of the nineteenth century roused European interest, but it was not until the French occupation of Algeria that the *original was found.

In mere extent of his travels Ibn Baṭṭūṭa surpassed all ancient and medieval travellers. That his work should contain errors was inevitable, especially as the loss of his notes at the hand of pirates in the Indian Ocean compelled him to trust entirely to his memory; but they are so few and rarely important that the work ranks as an authority for the social and cultural history of post-Mongol Islam. His very faults are, if faults at all, those of his age; his sincerity is above suspicion. The book has, too, a literary interest of its own. Ibn Juzayy, it is true, decked it out with poetical citations, purple passages from Ibn Jubair and others, and naïve interpolations of his own, but the work remains substantially a simple narrative, full of racy incident and touches of humour, without pretensions to style, and interspersed with anecdotes that throw an abundance of light on the manners of the times.

At Lādhiqīya we embarked on a large galley belonging to the Genoese, the name of whose owner was Martelmīn [? Bartolomeo], and made for the country of the Turks which is known by the name of 'the land of Rūm'. It is so called from the Rūm (Greeks), because it was their land in ancient times. . . . There are now many Christians there, living under the protection of the Turcoman Muslims. We sailed for ten days with a favouring wind; the Christian [owner] was most kind to us and took no passage-money from us. On the tenth day we reached the city of 'Alaya, which is on the frontiers of Rūm. This country called Rūm is one of the fairest countries on earth; in it God has united all the good features dispersed amongst other lands. Its people are the most beautiful in form, the cleanest in dress, the most delicate in food, and the most bountiful of all God's creatures, and for that reason the proverb goes 'Syria for blessing and Rūm for kindness'. Whenever we halted in this land, in hospice or private house, our neighbours both men and women—these do not veil themselves—came to enquire after us, and when we journeyed away from them, they bade us farewell as though they were our own family and household, and you would see the women weeping in sorrow at our parting.[1]

We are particularly well furnished with historical works on the Berber dynasties of north Africa, the best known and one of the most valuable being the **History of the Almóhads* by 'Abdal-Wāḥid of Marrakush (1185–?). All these local historians are overshadowed by 'Abdar-Raḥmān Ibn Khaldūn (1332–1406) of Tunis, the chief historian of his age and the inventor of a new science of history. We know from his own *autobiography the details of his adventurous political career in north-west Africa, how difficult it was for him to find the leisure he craved for his literary pursuits, and how eventually he made his way to Cairo, where he spent his last years in distinguished service as a *qāḍī*. His great historical work (*The Book of Examples*) was begun in 1377 and subsequently revised several times. It contains an introduction, a résumé of general Muhammadan history (largely abridged from Ibn al-Athīr), supplementary chapters on more recent develop-

[1] A footnote at least is due to a later traveller, al-Wazzān of Fez (d. after 1526), who, after his capture by Christian corsairs, settled in Italy, and on his conversion adopted the name of John Leo. The Arabic original (or notes) of his work is lost, but in its author's Italian *version it remained the chief authority for European works on Africa until the end of the eighteenth century.

ments in the East, and finally a detailed *history of the Berbers and north African dynasties. As a writer of historical chronicles his true valuation has yet to be reached; his independent work will certainly stand comparison with that of any other Muslim historian, however much it may fall short of the standard he himself demanded. But it is on his comprehensive **Introduction* that his fame most truly rests. Coming at the end of eight centuries of Muslim political development, and from his own experience familiar with the raw material of history in north Africa, he attempted to group all its outward phenomena under general principles and thus reached, for the first time (so far as we know) in human literature, a philosophic conception of history.

Wise and ignorant are at one in appreciating history, since in its external aspect it is no more than narratives telling us how circumstances revolutionize the affairs of men, but in its internal aspect it involves an accurate perception of the causes and origins of phenomena. For this reason it is based on and deeply rooted in philosophy, worthy to be reckoned among its branches.

Human society in its various manifestations shows certain inherent features by which all narratives must be controlled. . . . The historian who relies solely upon tradition and who has no thorough understanding of the principles governing the normal course of events, the fundamental rules of the art of government, the nature of civilization and the characteristics of human society is seldom secure against straying from the highway of truth. . . . All traditional narratives must invariably be referred back to general principles and controlled by reference to fundamental rules.

Ibn Khaldūn was singularly free from political, theological, or philosophical prejudices, and so was under less temptation than the majority of historians to make the facts fit a preconceived theory. He saw rightly that the course of history is governed by the balance of two forces, which for him were nomadic and settled life. He identified, therefore, the science of history with the science of civilization, and having established his general theory devoted the greater part of his prolegomena to tracing in detail the various developments of civilization in its religious, administrative, economic, and artistic and scientific aspects. In all this, of course, his work refers to and has value for only the political conditions of his age and community, but for those it is inestimable.

Of the numerous later histories written by natives of north-west Africa (most of which have been translated into French) only one has a wider interest in Arabic literature. In 1630 al-Maqqarī (1591–1632) of Tlemsen wrote, at the request of some Damascene scholars, a *history of Spain and biography of Ibn al-Khaṭīb (p. 150). The first part of his book contains a fund of information on the political and literary history of Andaluŝia, extracted largely from the early works now lost, and unless some happy chance restores these to us, will always be our chief authority for the springtide of Spanish–Arabic culture.

§ 3. A.D. 1517–1800

After the Ottoman conquests a profound intellectual lethargy seems to settle on the Arab lands. How far it may be explained by historical or geographical conditions, by economic impoverishment, or by the deadening influence of a stereotyped circle of thought, are questions outside our range. The contrast with the awakening mind of Europe, it may be, casts an unduly dark shadow over the sixteenth to the nineteenth centuries; there was no violent dislocation, and literary composition seems to have continued almost as actively as before, but only a pitiably small handful of works stand out from the monotonous mass of mediocrity.

The biographical tradition continued to flourish not only in Syria, with centennial dictionaries for each century, but also in Yemen and Morocco, where its most notable representative was Aḥmad Bābā of Timbuktū (d. 1627). Historical writing, by contrast, makes a poor showing with a few local chronicles. Ṣūfism was the most significant cultural feature of the age and provided its most noteworthy writers: the Egyptian ash-Shaʿrānī (d. 1565), who combined Ṣūfī biography with fantastic flights of mystical experience, and the Syrian ʿAbd al-Ghanī of Nāblus (d. 1731), a prolific author who originated a new kind of mystical travel-literature in rhymed prose, and a gifted poet as well. As in earlier periods of decline of the High Arabic tradition, popular poetry in local dialect gained some recognition, notably a sustained masterpiece of satire by the Egyptian ash-Shirbīnī (d. 1687).

With such poverty in its homelands, the chief interest of Arabic literature now lies, rather paradoxically, in the wide extension of its geographical area. The upheavals of the fourteenth century had resulted in the spread of Islam in central Africa, India and Malaysia, China, Russia, and eastern Europe. With Islam came the Arabic Koran and Arabic theological literature; Arabic outposts were thus founded in the new territories and, especially where there was no existing literary language, supplied the medium of learned communications. In India, although Persian was the official language of the Muhammadan courts, there appeared from time to time a few non-theological works, and even poetry, written in Arabic, including two histories, *one of the introduction of Islam into Malabar and the struggle with the Portuguese, the other of the kingdom of Gujarat. Even in the Malay Archipelago a few theological works were written in Arabic. In China, on the other hand, the Muhammadan community, although Arabic works were studied, wrote in Chinese only.

The literature of the Turkish lands in Anatolia and eastern Europe stood from the beginning in much closer dependence on Persian than on Arabic models, but the Ottoman absorption of the Arab provinces appears to have led to a slightly more extensive use of Arabic for general literary purposes. There is a fairly large number of Arabic works written by Turks in prose, rhymed prose, and verse, the best known being a dictionary of Turkish savants by Ṭāshköprüzāda (d. 1560), an elaborate *bibliography of Arabic, Persian, and Turkish works by Ḥājjī Khalīfa (d. 1658), a secretary in the War Department at Constantinople, and a valuable general chronicle by Munajjim Bāshī (d. 1702).

Islam penetrated into central Africa both from the East and from the West. For many centuries Arab trading stations had been established along the east coast as far as Sofala, and in course of time large Muslim colonies grew up in Zanzibar and the continent. We possess a number of works written in these colonies, including several histories of the trading stations themselves, and an important narrative of the struggles between Muslims and Christians in Abyssinia written about 1540 by a Somali Arab surnamed *ʿArabfaqīh. From Morocco Islam penetrated into the Niger territories in the eleventh century, and there, too, an Arabic historical literature came into existence in the sixteenth century, the most interesting work being a political and ethnographical account of the Songhay kingdom, written in 1656 by *as-Saʿdī, a native of Timbuktū.

The prestige of the college-mosque of al-Azhar drew scholars and students from all these outposts of Islam to Cairo. Out of their number there emerged in the second half of the eighteenth century, under the patronage of the Mamlūk Beys, two personalities who rank in their own fields with the greatest in Arabic literature. From the Somali coast came the ancestors of al-Jabartī (d. 1825), whose *chronicle of Egypt from about 1700 to 1820 has few rivals in Arabic for precision, breadth, and insight. The other, Sayyid Murtaḍā (d. 1791), was of south-Arabian parentage and Indian birth. Of his philological learning an enduring monument remains in the valuable commentary (with the curious name of *The Bride's Crown*) which he wrote to one of the standard earlier lexicons, but of far greater significance was his re-edition, also with an exhaustive commentary, of Ghazālī's *Iḥyā* (p. 121). The effect of his work, in which he threw over all pedantic and slavish dependence on earlier writers and went direct to his sources, combined with his personal energy and enthusiasm, was to arouse a new interest in learning, and to bring back into the benumbed religious conscience of Islam the moral earnestness and vigorous personal faith of Ghazālī. It was time, for the crucial hour of Islam was striking.

EPILOGUE

FOR the Muslim world, and especially its Arab lands, the nineteenth century ushered in an era of storm and stress, both from within and without. Napoleon's meteoric invasion of Egypt in 1798 tore aside the veil of apathy which had cut them off from the new life of Europe and gave the death-blow to medievalism. Slowly at first, but with increasing momentum, the literature and the ideas of the western world gained a lodgement, and stimulated the production of a new Modern Arabic literature.

Internally, the new literature received its impetus from the interaction of two movements, both represented simultaneously in Syria and in Egypt. The first movement aimed, paradoxical as it may seem, at a revival of classical Arabic and produced a remarkable series of literary works directly inspired or influenced by classical models. The ambition of their authors was to rescue the Arabic language from its degeneration in the preceding centuries and to restore the heritage of classical literary art. Their efforts were powerfully seconded by a pleiad of poets in Egypt and Iraq, who married a new range of patriotic and contemporary themes with the old measures and modes of expression of Arabic poetry, and by a number of publicists educated in the religious schools, the outstanding figure among whom was *Shaikh Muḥammad ʿAbduh (1849–1905).

The labours of this school polished the instrument with which the writers of the second movement were experimenting for the conveyance of western themes and techniques. The viceroy of Egypt, Muḥammad ʿAlī (d. 1849), had set up a bureau for the translation of technical works, especially of military and medical science, but more influential in transmitting the new ideas were a group of Lebanese scholars who were in contact with the western educational missions in Beirut. These men were also the creators of a new periodical press and a modern journalistic medium; these, transplanted to Egypt, at first still largely under Lebanese direction but soon followed by a vigorous native Egyptian production, proved to be the real forcing-bed of modern Arabic literature. During the last decades of the nineteenth century and the first decade of the twentieth, the Egyptian press was the theatre in which literary reputations were made and literary Arabic adapted to modern themes. At the same time a school of Syro-American writers were producing in their Arabic journals in the New World new forms of the literary essay and Whitmanesque 'prose poems'. Although they were widely read and celebrated in their native country, the ingenuous freedom with which they handled the classical linguistic structure found only moderate favour with the literary public.

In addition to journalism and original writing, a vital part in the development of modern Arabic literature was played by the translation of western literary works. These served not only as exercises in expanding the range of Arabic literary expression, but also as models, since not a few translators tried their hands at original compositions of the same kinds. The most ambitious was the attempt to develop a dramatic literature, modelled on the classical French dramatists, but it cannot be said that the Arabic drama achieved much success in the nineteenth century. On the other hand, some progress was made with the novel, particularly in the series of historical novels in the manner of Scott produced by the indefatigable journalist, essayist, and historian *Jirji Zaidān (1861–1914).

During the past four decades this intensive effort and experiment have borne fruit in a modern literature that expresses the contemporary social and intellectual interests of the Arab peoples. The way was finally opened by the short story, followed by the novel of manners and the literary drama. Beginning with an autobiographical work by Ṭāhā Ḥusain, **The Days* (1926), increasing depth in social and psychological analysis has been matched by more flexible methods of presentation and stylistic devices. The drama also has benefited from these technical advances, and has found in *Tawfīq al-Ḥakīm a major exponent, both in literary drama and in plays on modern social themes. All of these productions, however, short stories, novels, and plays, remain bounded by the horizons and conventions of the Arab world; when translated into other languages they are often more interesting as social documents than as literary achievements.

Alongside these new arts, a highly significant role is being played by the literary essay. Broadly speaking, the aim of the essayists has been not only to present critical evaluations of both classical Arabic and western literature, as well as social criticism in general, but to relate the values of the Arab cultural tradition, in the widest sense, to the modern world. The majority, unlike their medieval predecessors, are far more concerned with content than with form; their approach to language is, like that of the short-story writers and the novelists, functional. The total outcome of these varieties of prose writing has, therefore, been to create an instrument that meets all contemporary needs with vigour and precision; but, inasmuch as precision in Arabic requires a certain degree of elegance, not without aesthetic qualities that vary with the diverse tastes of the writers.

In contrast to this deliberate functionalism in prose, the poetry of the same period has moved further and further away from the conventions of classical poetry towards the freedoms of modern western poetry. The intensity of political and social aspirations could not fail, on the one hand, to inspire an output in which traditional themes and imagery were applied to modern situations with stirring effect. At the same time most of the younger generation of poets have been experimenting with the creation of a psychological poetry that breaks with the poetic tradition not only in new strophic and rhythmic forms, but also in linguistic nuances and contextual associations. In this respect, many Arabic poets, although more 'international' in technique and themes than Arabic prose-writers, seem content (like some western poets) to live in their own private worlds.

BIBLIOGRAPHY

SELECT LIST OF BOOKS OF REFERENCE AND TRANSLATION FROM ARABIC WORKS IN ENGLISH AND OTHER WESTERN LANGUAGES[1]

CHAPTER 1

C. Brockelmann: *Geschichte der arabischen Literatur* (second edition, 2 vols., Leiden, 1943–9). Bio-bibliographical summaries; standard reference work.

R. A. Nicholson: (1) *A Literary History of the Arabs* (London, 1907). A delightful work, of special value for poetry.

(2) *Eastern Poetry and Prose* (Cambridge, 1922). Contains representative extracts from 32 Arabic authors.

Carra de Vaux: *Les Penseurs de l'Islam* (5 small vols., Paris, 1921–5).

D. B. Macdonald: *Development of Muslim . . . Theology* (London, 1903, &c.). An invaluable and simply written introduction to Muslim thought.

G. Wiet: *Grandeur de l'Islam* (Paris, 1961). Selected translations in French.

B. Lewis: *The Arabs in History* (London, 1950, &c.). Up-to-date summary.

C. M. Doughty: *Travels in Arabia Deserta* (London (repr.), 1922). The standard work on Arabia and Bedouin life.

CHAPTER 2

Th. Nöldeke: Article 'Semitic Languages' in *Encyclopaedia Britannica*, eleventh edition (*Die semitischen Sprachen*, Leipzig, 1887).

[1] For articles on individual writers with translations from their works see J. D. Pearson, *Index Islamicus*, Cambridge, 1958.

CHAPTER 3

Sir Charles Lyall: (1) *Translations of Ancient Arabic Poetry* (London, 1885), chiefly from the *Ḥamāsa* of Abū Tammām. Sir Charles Lyall is unquestionably the most successful translator of the ancient poets in English, and his introduction to this work is invaluable.

(2) Translations of the *Mufaḍḍalīyāt* (Oxford, 1918), the dīwān of ʿAbīd b. al-Abraṣ (Leiden, 1913), and of several other early poets.

W. A. Clouston: *Arabian Poetry for English Readers* (Glasgow, 1881). This work reprints Sir William Jones's prose translations of the *Muʿallaqāt*, a miscellany of shorter poems of all periods translated by J. D. Carlyle, prose translations of several important odes by J. W. Redhouse, and a number of other pieces, with introductions and notes.

Fr. Rückert: *Die Hamâsa* (Stuttgart, 1846). A masterly version, which contains also translations of many other poems.

Muʿallaqāt: (1) W. S. Blunt, *Seven Golden Odes of Pagan Arabia* (London, 1903).

(2) A. J. Arberry, *The Seven Odes* (London, 1957).

Al-Khansā: G. Gabrieli, *I tempi . . . e il canzoniere della poetessa araba al-Ḫansā'* (Rome, 1944).

Imru'ul-Qais: *Diwan d'Amro'lkais*, tr. MacGuckin de Slane (Paris, 1837).

Ta'abbaṭa Sharrā: translations in Lyall (1) and Nicholson (1) and (2).

Shanfarā: translation in Wiet, *Grandeur de l'Islam.*

Nābigha: *Dîwân* . . ., tr. Hartwig Derenbourg (Paris, 1869).

Several *dīwāns* of minor poets have also been translated.

CHAPTER 4

Muḥammad: (1) W. M. Watt: *Muhammad at Mecca* (Oxford, 1953); *Muhammad at Medina* (Oxford, 1956).

(2) Tor Andrae: *Mohammed, The Man and his Faith* (London, 1936).

Koran: (1) A. J. Arberry: *The Koran Interpreted* (2 vols., London, 1955). An elegant modern translation.

KORAN: (2) R. BLACHÈRE: *Le Coran* (Paris, 1957). A more critical annotated translation, with an index.

KA'B B. ZUHAIR: *Bānat Su'ād* (1) Tr. R. Basset (Algiers, 1910). (2) Tr. R. A. Nicholson in (2) above.

LABĪD: *Die Gedichte des Lebîd*, übers. A. Hüber (Leiden, 1891).

FARAZDAQ: *Divan* . . ., tr. R. Boucher (Paris, 1870–5).

'OMAR B. ABĪ RABĪ'A: W. G. Palgrave, 'The Poet 'Omar' in *Essays on Eastern Questions* (London, 1872).

CHAPTER 5. § 1

SĪBAWAIH: *Sîbawaihis Buch* . . ., übers. G. Jahn (Berlin, 1894).

Shu'ūbīya: I. Goldziher, *Muhammedanische Studien* (Halle, 1888), pp. 147–216.

Kalīla wa-Dimna: tr. A. Miquel (Paris, 1957).

ABŪ YŪSUF: *Le Livre de l'Impôt Foncier*, tr. E. Fagnan (Paris, 1921).

IBN ISḤĀQ: *The Life of Muhammad*, tr. A. Guillaume (London, 1955).

IBN HISHĀM: *Das Leben Mohammeds*, übers. G. Weil (Stuttgart, 1864).

WĀQIDĪ: *Muhammad in Medîna* (abridged tr. of *Kitāb al-Maghāzī* by), J. Wellhausen (Berlin, 1882).

ABŪ NUWĀS: *Dîwân*, deutsch von W. von Kremer (Vienna, 1855).

IBN AL-MU'TAZZ: C. Lang, *Mu'taḍid als Prinz und Regent*, Z.D.M.G., vols. xl and xli.

Arabic philosophers and scientists: G. SARTON, *Introduction to the History of Science* (3 vols., Baltimore, 1927–48).

KHWĀRIZMĪ: *The Algebra of Mohammed ben Musa*, ed. and tr. F. Rosen (London, 1831).

THEOLOGY OF ARISTOTLE, tr. G.L.Lewis, in *Plotini Opera*, tom. ii, ed. P. Henry and H.-R. Schwyzer (Paris-Brussels, 1959).

JĀḤIẒ: (1) *Le Livre des Avares*, tr. C. Pellat (Paris, 1951).
(2) 'The Merits of the Turks', tr. Harley Walker (*Journal of the Royal Asiatic Society*, 1915).

PSEUDO-JĀḤIẒ: (1) *Kitāb al-Maḥāsin wa'l-Aḍdād*, 2. Teil, übers. O. Rescher (Stuttgart, 1922).
(2) *Le Livre de la Couronne*, tr. C. Pellat (Paris, 1954).

IBN QUTAIBA: (1) *'Uyūn al-Akhbār*, bk. IV, tr. L. Kopf (Leiden, 1949).

IBN QUTAIBA: (2) *Introduction au Livre de la Poésie et des Poètes*, ed. and tr. with an Introduction by Gaudefroy-Demombynes (Paris, 1947).

§ 2

ṢŪFISM: (1) A. J. Arberry, *Sufism* (London, 1950). A short introductory survey.

(2) L. Massignon, *Essai sur les origines du Lexique technique de la Mystique musulmane* (Paris, 1922); includes a valuable summary of the development of Ṣūfism and sufistic schools during the first three centuries.

MUḤĀSIBI: M. Smith, *An Early Mystic of Baghdad* (London, 1935).

RĀBIʿA: M. Smith, *Rābiʿa the Mystic* (Cambridge, 1928).

ASHʿARĪ: (1) R. J. McCarthy, S.J., *The Theology of al-Ashʿarī* (Beirut, 1953).

(2) *Al-Ibānah*, tr. W. C. Klein (New Haven, Conn., 1940).

ḤALLĀJ: L. Massignon, *La Passion d'... al-Ḥallāj* (Paris, 1922).

QUSHAIRĪ: R. Hartmann. *Al-Ḳuschairîs Darstellung des Ṣufîtums* (Berlin, 1914).

TRADITION: (1) I. Goldziher, *Muhammedanische Studien*, 2. Theil (Halle, 1890), is the standard monograph on the subject.

(2) A. Guillaume, *The Traditions of Islam* (Oxford, 1924); a useful introduction, based on the preceding.

(3) W. Goldsack, *Selections from Muḥammadan Traditions* (Madras, 1923); taken from the very popular fourteenth-century compilation called *Mishkāt al-Maṣābīḥ*.

BUKHĀRĪ: *Les Traditions islamiques*, tr. O. Houdas et W. Marçais (Paris, 1903–14).

BALĀDHURĪ: (1) *The Origins of the Islamic State*, tr. P. K. Ḥitti and F. C. Murgotten (New York, 1916–24).

(2) L. della Vida, *Il Califfo Muʿawiya I* (Rome, 1938). Extracted from *The Genealogies of the Nobles*.

ṬABARĪ:[1] (1) *Geschichte der Perser und Araber zur Zeit der Sassaniden*, übers. . . . Th. Nöldeke (Leiden, 1879).

[1] The Persian abridgement of Ṭabarî's Annales (*Chronique de Tabarî*, tr. by M. H. Zotenberg, 4 vols., Paris, 1867–74) gives a very imperfect idea of the Arabic original.

TABARĪ: (2) *The Reign of al-Muʿtasim* (833–842), tr. E. Marin (New Haven, Conn., 1951).
MASʿŪDĪ: (1) *Les Prairies d'Or* . . ., tr. C. Barbier de Meynard et Pavet de Courteille (Paris, 1861–77).
(2) *Le Livre de l'Avertissement et de la Revision*, tr. B. Carra de Vaux (Paris, 1897).
YAʿQŪBĪ: *Les Pays*, tr. G. Wiet (Cairo, 1937).
IṢṬAKHRĪ: *The Oriental Geography of Ebn Haukal*, tr. [from a Persian MS. combining both works] Sir Wm. Ouseley (London, 1800).
IBN YAʿQŪB: G. Jacob, *Ein arabischer Berichterstatter aus dem 10. Jahrh.* (Berlin, 1896).
IBN FAḌLĀN: 'Relation du Voyage d'I. F.', tr. M. Canard, in *Annales de l'Institut des Études Orientales*, vol. XVI (Algiers, 1958).
Chain of Histories: (1) *Relations des voyages faits par les Arabes* . . ., tr. Reinaud (Paris, 1845). An English version exists (London, 1733) of the older translation by Renaudot.
(2) *Voyage du marchand Sulayman en Inde et en Chine* . . ., tr. G. Ferrand (Paris, 1922).
Livre des Merveilles de l'Inde: tr. L. M. Devic (Leiden, 1886) (English translation by P. Quennell, London, 1928).
L'Abrégé des Merveilles, tr. B. Carra de Vaux (Paris, 1897).
RĀZĪ (Muḥammad b. Zakarīyā'): A. J. Arberry, *The Spiritual Physick of Rhazes* (London, 1950).

§ 3

JURJĀNĪ: *Geheimnisse der Wortkunst*, übers. H. Ritter (Wiesbaden, 1959).
Motenebbi, der größte arabische Dichter . . ., übers. J. von Hammer (Vienna, 1824).
Abū Firās, ein arabischer Dichter und Held, übers. R. Dvořak (Leiden, 1895).
FĀRĀBĪ: (1) *Philosophische Abhandlungen*, übers. F. Dieterici (Leiden, 1892).
(2) *Der Musterstaat* . . ., übers. F. Dieterici (Leiden, 1900).
ABU'L-ʿALĀ: (1) R. A. Nicholson, *Studies in Islamic Poetry* (Cambridge, 1921).
(2) *The Letters of Abu'l-ʿAlā*, tr. D. S. Margoliouth (Oxford, 1898).

MISKAWAIH: D. S. Margoliouth, *The Eclipse of the Abbasid Caliphate* (Oxford, 1921); contains translations of vols. v and vi of the *Experiences of the Nations* with two continuations by later writers.

TANŪKHĪ: *The Table-Talk of a Mesopotamian Judge* (i.e. vol. i of *The Collection of Histories*), tr. D. S. Margoliouth (London, 1922).

ABSHĪHĪ: *Al-Mostaṭraf*, tr. par G. Rat (Paris, 1899–1902).

MĀWARDĪ: *Les Statuts gouvernementaux*, tr. E. Fagnan (Algiers, 1915).

'ALĪ (attributed to): *La Kasîda ez-Zaïnabiyya*, tr. A. Raux (Paris, 1907).

IKHWĀN AṢ-ṢAFĀ: *Die Propaedeutik* (*Logik, Naturanschauung, Anthropologie, Lehre von der Weltseele*) *der Araber im X. Jahrh* . . ., übers. F. Dieterici (Berlin and Leipzig, 1861–72).

BADĪ' AZ-ZAMĀN HAMADHĀNĪ: (1) *The Maqámát*, tr. W. Prendergast (Madras, 1915).
(2) *Choix de Maqāmāt*, tr. R. Blachère, etc. (Paris, 1957).

THA'ALIBĪ: (1) *Les Rois de Perse* . . ., tr. H. Zotenberg (Paris, 1900).
(2) C. Barbier de Meynard, 'Tableau littéraire de la Khorassan [tr. from book iv of *Yatîmat ad-Dahr*]', *Journal Asiatique*, 1853, 1854.

'UTBĪ: *The Kitāb al-Yamīnī*, tr. J. Reynolds (London, 1858).

AL-BĪRŪNĪ: (1) *The Chronology of Ancient Nations*, tr. E. Sachau (London, 1879).
(2) *India*, tr. E. Sachau (London, 1888).

IBN SĪNĀ: (1) A. J. Arberry, *Avicenna on Theology* (London, 1951). Extracts.
(2) A.-M. Goichon, *Livre des Directives et Remarques* (Paris, 1951).
(3) H. Corbin, *Avicenne et le Récit visionnaire* (Teheran, 1954).
(4) F. Rahman: *Avicenna's Psychology* (London, 1952).

For Spanish and Sicilian poetry in general, the standard work is A. F. von Schack, *Poesie und Kunst der Araber in Spanien und Sicilien* (2nd ed., Stuttgart, 1877).

IBN ZAIDŪN: A. Cour, *Un poète arabe d'Andalousie* (Constantine, 1920); includes translations of some fifty poems and of the *Epistle to Ibn 'Abdūs*.

'ALĪ AṬ-ṬABARĪ: *The Book of Religion and Empire*, tr. A. Mingana (London, 1922).
IBN ḤAZM: *The Ring of the Dove*, tr. A. J. Arberry (London, 1953).
BAGHDĀDĪ: *Moslem Sects and Schisms*, tr. K. Seeley (Columbia, 1920).

CHAPTER 6

GHAZĀLĪ: (1) *Streitschrift . . . gegen die Bāṭinijja-Sekte*, ed. with analysis by I. Goldziher (Leiden, 1916).
(2) T. J. de Boer, *Die Widersprüche der Philosophie nach al-Ġazzālī und ihr Ausgleich durch Ibn Roshd* (Strassburg, 1894).
(3) W. M. Watt, *The Faith and Practice of Al-Ghazālī* (London, 1953). Contains a translation of the *Rescuer from Error*.
(4) Hans Bauer, *Islamische Ethik* (Halle, 1917–22); translations of books 12–14 of Ghazālī's *Iḥyā*.
(5) *La Perle précieuse*, tr. L. Gautier (Geneva, 1878); a popular treatise on eschatology.
(6) *Mishkāt al-Anwār*, tr. W. H. T. Gairdner (London, 1924); a mystic treatise on Light.
ZAMAKHSHARĪ: *Les Colliers d'Or*, tr. C. Barbier de Meynard (Paris, 1876).
ḤARĪRĪ: *The Assemblies*, tr. T. Chenery (London, 1867); continued by F. Steingass (London, 1898). Two *maqāmāt* are translated into English rhymed prose in R. A. Nicholson (2) above.
ṬUGHRĀ'Ī: *Lāmīyat al-'Ajam*, tr. by J. W. Redhouse in Clouston, op. cit.
IBN AL-JAWZĪ: *The Devil's Delusion*, tr. D. S. Margoliouth, in *Islamic Culture*, vols. 9–12 (Hyderabad, 1935–8).
NASAWĪ: *Histoire du Sultan Djelal ed-Din*, tr. O. Houdas (Paris, 1895).
SHAHRISTĀNĪ: *Religionsparteien und Philosophenschule*, übers. Th. Haarbrücker (Halle, 1850–1).
YĀQŪT: (1) *Introductory Chapters of Mu'jam al-Buldān*, tr. W. Jwaideh (Leiden, 1959).
(2) *Dictionnaire . . . de la Perse*, tr. C. Barbier de Meynard (Paris, 1861).

IBN AL-QALĀNISĪ: *Damas de 1075 à 1154*, tr. R. Le Tourneau (Beirut, 1952).

USĀMA B. MUNQIDH: *An Arab-Syrian Gentleman*, tr. P. K. Hitti (New York, 1929).

IBN AL-ʿARABĪ: *Tarjumān al-Ashwāq*, tr. R. A. Nicholson (London, 1911).

ʿOMAR B. AL-FĀRIḌ: R. A. Nicholson, *Studies in Islamic Mysticism* (Cambridge, 1921).

BAHĀ AD-DĪN ZUHAIR: *Dīwān*, tr. E. H. Palmer (Cambridge, 1877).

BAHĀ AD-DĪN of MOSUL: *Life of Saladin*, tr. C. R. Conder (London, 1892).

ABŪ SHĀMA: *Livre des Deux Jardins*, tr. B. de Meynard
IBN AL-ATHĪR: (1) *Histoire des Atabecs de Mosul*, tr. MacGuckin de Slane
(2) *Extrait de la . . . Kamel*, tr. J. T. Reinaud et C. F. Defrémery
} *Recueil des Historiens des Croisades . . .* Historiens orientaux, tomes 1, 2, 4, 5 (Paris, 1872, &c.).

(3) *Annales du Maghrib et de l'Espagne*, tr. E. Fagnan [from the *Kāmil*] (Algiers, 1901).

AL-MAKĪN: *Historia Saracenica . . .*, lat. redd. Th. Erpenius (Leiden, 1625; English version by S. Purchas, London, 1626).

ABU'L-FIDĀ: (1) *De Vita . . . Muhammedis . . .*, lat. vert. J. Gagnier (Oxford, 1723).
(2) *Annales Moslemici . . .*, lat. fecit J. J. Reiske (Leipzig, 1754 and 1778).

ʿABD AL-LAṬĪF: *Description de l'Égypte*, tr. S. de Sacy (Paris, 1808).

IBN KHALLIKĀN: *Biographical Dictionary*, tr. MacGuckin de Slane (4 vols., Paris, 1842–71).

IDRĪSĪ: (1) *Géographie*, tr. P. A. Jaubert (Paris, 1836–40).
(2) *Description de l'Afrique et de l'Espagne*, tr. R. Dozy et M. J. de Goeje (Leyden, 1866).
(3) *Passages relating to India, etc.*, tr. S. Maqbul Ahmad (Leiden, 1960).

IBN ẒAFAR: *Solwan, or Waters of Comfort*, tr. M. Amari (London, 1852).

IBN QUZMĀN: A. R. Nykl, *El Cancionero de Aben Guzmán* (Madrid, 1933).
IBN ṬUFAIL: *Hayy ben Yaqdhan*, tr. Léon Gauthier (Algiers, 1900).
IBN RUSHD: (1) *Die Metaphysik des Averroes*, übers. M. Horten (Halle, 1912).
(2) *Averroes' Tahafut al-Tahafut*, tr. S. van den Bergh (London, 1954).
(3) *Averroes on the Harmony of Religion and Philosophy*, tr. G. F. Hourani (London, 1961).
IBN SABʿĪN: 'Correspondance du Philosophe Soufī Ibn Sabʿin . . ., tr. A. F. Mehren (in *Journal Asiatique*, 1880).
IBN SAʿID: *The Pennants*, tr. A. J. Arberry (Cambridge, 1953).
IBN JUBAIR: *Travels*, tr. R. J. C. Broadhurst (London, 1952).

CHAPTER 7

IBN AT-ṬIQṬAQĀ: *Al-Fakhrī* (1) tr. E. Amar (Paris, 1910).
(2) tr. C. E. J. Whitting (London, 1947).
BUṢĪRĪ: *La Bordah*, tr. R. Basset (Paris, 1894). English translation by J. W. Redhouse in Clouston, op. cit.
DIMISHQĪ: *Manuel de la Cosmographie du Moyen Âge*, tr. A. F. Mehren (Copenhagen, 1874).
ABU'L-FIDĀ: *Géographie* . . ., tr. Reinaud et S. Guyard (Paris, 1848, 1883).
QALQASHANDĪ: (1) *La Syrie à l'Époque des Mamelouks*, par Gaudefroy-Demombynes (Paris, 1923).
(2) *Die Geographie und Verwaltung von Ägypten*, übers. F. Wüstenfeld (Göttingen, 1879).
IBN TAIMĪYA: *Contributions à une Étude de la Méthodologie canonique*, tr. H. Laoust (Cairo, 1939).
MAQRĪZĪ: (1) *Histoire des Sultans Mamelouks de l'Égypte*, tr. E. Quatremère (Paris, 1837–45).
(2) *Description . . . de l'Égypte*, tr. U. Bouriant (Paris, 1895–1900, incomplete).
IBN ʿARABSHĀH: *Histoire du grand Tamerlan*, tr. P. Vattier (Paris, 1658).
SUYŪṬĪ: *History of the Caliphs*, tr. H. S. Jarrett (Calcutta, 1881).

Thousand and One Nights: (1) *Les Mille et Une Nuits*, tr. M. Galland (Hague, 1714, &c.).
(2) Complete English translation by J. Payne (13 vols., London, 1882–9).
(3) Abridged English translation by E. W. Lane (3 vols., London, 1839–41).

Hundred. and One Nights: tr. Gaudefroy-Demombynes (Paris, n.d.).

Romance of 'Antar: tr. [from the Syrian version] T. Hamilton (London, 1820).

Arabische Schattenspiele, E. Littmann (Berlin, 1901).

IBN HUDHAIL: *La Parure des Cavaliers* . . ., tr. L. Mercier (Paris, 1924).

IBN BAṬṬŪṬA: (1) *Les Voyages d'Ibn Batouta*, éd. & tr. C. Defrémery et B. R. Sanguinetti (4 vols., Paris, 1853, &c.).
(2) *Travels of Ibn Baṭṭūṭa*, tr. H. A. R. Gibb (Hakluyt Society, 1958, proceeding).
(3) *The Travels of Ibn Batūta*, tr. from the abridged Arabic manuscripts, by S. Lee (London, 1829).

LEO AFRICANUS: Jean-Léon l'Africain, *Description de l'Afrique*, tr. A. Épaulard (2 vols., Paris, 1956).

IBN KHALDŪN: (1) *Prolégomènes*. . ., tr. MacGuckin de Slane (3 vols., Paris, 1863–8; contains also Ibn Khaldūn's *Autobiography*).
(2) *The Muqaddimah*, tr. F. Rosenthal (3 vols., New York, 1958).
(3) *Histoire des Berbères* . . ., tr. MacGuckin de Slane (4 vols., Algiers, 1852; revised ed., Paris, 1925–56).

MAQQARĪ: *The History of the Mohammedan Dynasties in Spain*, tr. Pascual de Gayzangos (London, 1840).

Tuḥfat al-Mujāhidīn, tr. M. J. Rowlandson (London, 1833).

ḤĀJJĪ KHALĪFA: *Lexicon bibliographicum* . . ., lat. vert. G. Flügel (7 vols., Leipzig, 1835–58).

'ARABFAQĪH: *Conquête de l'Abyssinie*, tr. R. Basset (Paris, 1897–9).

SA'DĪ: *Ta'rīkh as-Soudān*, tr. O. Houdas (Paris, 1900).

JABARTĪ: (1) *Merveilles biographiques et historiques* . . ., tr. Chefik Mansour Bey, &c. (Cairo, 1888–94).
(2) *Journal d'Abdurrahman Gabarti* . . ., tr. A. Cardin (Paris, 1838).

EPILOGUE

MUḤAMMAD 'ABDUH: *Rissalat al-Tawhid*, tr. B. Michel (Paris, 1925).

JIRJĪ ZAIDAN: (1) *Der letzte Mameluck*, tr. M. Thilo (Barmen, 1917).

(2) *Omayyads and 'Abbāsids* (i.e. vol. iv of the *History of Islamic Civilization*), tr. D. S. Margoliouth (London, 1907).

T. ḤUSAIN: *An Egyptian Childhood*, tr. E. H. Paxton (London, 1932).

TAWFĪQ AL-ḤAKĪM: *Théâtre arabe* (Paris, 1950).

Modern Arabic Poetry: An anthology with English verse translations by A. J. Arberry (London, 1950).

INDEXES

I. LITERARY GENRES

II. AUTHORS, TITLES, ETC.

III. PLACE-NAMES, PEOPLES, RELIGIONS